Released

—A MEMOIR—

KL RHODES

Copyright © 2020 Kristin L. Rhodes
All rights reserved.
ISBN-13: 9798680573778

All rights reserved. No part of this publication may be reproduced, distributed, or transmitted in any form or by any means, including photocopying, recording, or other electronic or mechanical methods, without the prior written permission of the publisher, except in the case of brief quotations embodied in critical reviews and certain other noncommercial uses permitted by copyright law.

I dedicate this book to my husband. Thank you for wiping every tear, every soothing hug and every word of encouragement. I know this was not easy for you and you remained my rock through it all. I love you.

CONTENTS

Preface ix

Chapter 1	Innocence 1
Chapter 2	The New Kid 7
Chapter 3	Never the Same 13
Chapter 4	Confusion, Guilt and Anger 19
Chapter 5	The Haven 25
Chapter 6	College 33
Chapter 7	Trying Again 41
Chapter 8	Life Saver 49
Chapter 9	Contact 59
Chapter 10	The Arrangement 63
Chapter 11	The Awakening 71
Chapter 12	Getting Free 81
Chapter 13	Staying Strong 87
Chapter 14	Peaceful Road 99
Chapter 15	Released 105

PREFACE

Writing Released has been one of the most challenging things I have ever done. I remember talking with friends I had not spoken to in a while and they would ask how things were going. I always seemed to have another story to tell them about something that happened to me. Their response would be, "girl, you need to write a book." We would laugh it off and move on. As I started volunteering and working with young girls who were survivors like me or headed down a dangerous path, I was heartbroken that no one had taken the time to explain to them their options in life. No one had tried to reach out to them and guide them on a different path or helped them heal. I could not shake that pull of responsibility. I never want another woman to go through what I have gone through. I have a daughter I want to protect as much as I can. Whether I am on the preventative side or the healing side, I knew I had to do something.

I struggled for a long time about discussing the chain of events that took place in my life. I did not want to hurt anyone. I thought of my husband and children having to relive my pain. I am a private person and the thought of sharing my deepest, darkest moments with the world was unnerving. I also knew this was not about me.

The series of events were laid out for me in my life. It was easy for me to know where to begin. It was difficult reliving the abusive moments. Many things I had blocked out. As the writing process unfolded, the memories came flooding back. I had to remember I was in a safe place in my life and it was okay share this story. I do not have to look over my shoulder anymore.

Regardless of what happened during those times, I am not a person who wants to tear people down, so I chose to omit names. I am sure those who were in my life during those seasons, can connect the dots. What was important to me was getting the story out. I was careful to only discuss what was relevant to the story. I did not discuss other people who were in my life or situations that were happening simultaneously, that were not directly a part of these events to protect their privacy.

I stuck with the main life changing events but there were many little things I could have thrown in such as sexual harassment on the job. Guys I tried to get to know who lied about having wives and girlfriends. All these things had an impact on my depression, self – esteem and my decision to step away from relationships. The best thing I could have done was reconnect with God. That is how I healed and learned the truth of why my life was significant. My struggles were not for me. They were for next 13-year-old girl who is assaulted. The next college girl who has a controlling boyfriend. The next wife who finds herself on the receiving end of her husband's fists. They all need to know God has not abandoned them. Their life has purpose.

The Author

CHAPTER 1

Innocence

I am the youngest of five children. I have three brothers and one sister. Being the youngest, I was spoiled and sheltered. We lived in E. St. Louis, IL. I do not remember too much about living there since we moved when I was five years old. The only thing I do remember during that time, was my grandmother and the naps I took on her bed, waking up to Young and the Restless on television. My family told me how beautiful the city once was. It was a close knit predominantly black community. There were beautiful trees and parks. Lovely neighborhoods with manicured lawns. Everyone knew everyone. Great successes such as Jackie Joyner Kersee, Miles Davis and Tina Turner were from there. However, the city today no longer holds such beauty. There are many burned down, abandoned homes and there is a high crime rate. Unlike my siblings, I do not connect to this city as home.

My mother was a woman that was determined to make a good life for her family. She had children early, which caused her to drop out of school. When she had an opportunity, she got her GED, went to community college, transferred to St Louis University, and graduated top 10 in her class not only with her BA but with an MBA as well. While she was in school, she worked for Southwestern Bell Telephone Company. She started as a phone operator, and when she finished school, she was offered the opportunity to become an executive with the marketing department. Mom accepted the position which called for relocation. My mom had never lived away from her family before, but she knew it was time for a change. The city had started changing and my two oldest brothers had started getting into trouble. We moved to a nice suburban neighborhood in Landing, NJ. We were the only black family on the block, and even though I was too young to know the difference, my siblings were not too happy about it.

Most of our family was in Illinois, and although my siblings struggled with the drastic change in culture and not having any family in New Jersey, they eventually began establishing their lives. They started school, started meeting friends and joined activities. My sister was a cheerleader, dancer and in the band. I really looked up to her. My brothers were in various sports, such as baseball, basketball and football. After we moved to New Jersey, I started school. I was singing in the chorus when I was six years old and eventually ran track.

My mom tried to get me involved with other activities, but my love for singing and running won out. I was surprisingly good at track. I would place in the top three positions during every meet. My childhood life was good for me there, and I was happy. I had friends I played with, a fun school, and all my family around me.

My mom did not find us a church home, but I remember playing with my dolls while my mom watched Fred Price on television. That was when I was first introduced to pastors on TV. I watched my mom with her bible saying, "Amen!" in agreement. She would have bible study on the phone between "church service" during the week. I never thought of why my mom had church this way. I assumed it was because she was busy with work, and sometimes she would have to travel or take additional jobs.

When my oldest brother left for the Army, it did not have a major impact on me because we were not close. I missed him, but he was not home as long as everyone else. When my sister left, it was like my mom left. My sister was more like my mom, even if Mom was home. She did my hair, played with me, did my nails, washed my clothes, and made many of my meals. To me, she was "Mom." When my sister graduated from high school and entered the Air Force, I was devastated. We shared a room and being there without her was very scary at first. My mom redesigned my room and made it just for me. I remember my room color was changed to mauve and blue. It was pretty. I received a new comforter set, pictures on the walls, and curtains. It was almost like my sister was never there but, in my heart, I knew she had been. I would do all the dances I learned from her. Play dress up trying to look just as beautiful as she did for prom. Although she came home after basic training and during the time, she served bearing gifts, her stays was never long enough for me. It was always difficult to see her go.

I still had my friends to help me cope. There were a lot of children on my block. All I had to do was go outside, and we were in full swing playing hide and seek, red light green light, tag, making mud pies and just being kids. It was the best feeling in the world. I loved my school, and I loved my neighborhood. As the years went on, another one of my brothers graduated and headed off to the Army and the one who was still living at home was hardly there. I did not feel uncomfortable becoming a latch key kid. We lived in a neighborhood where parents were always watching, and as a child, I felt I could not be in a safer place. It was down to me, my 2nd to oldest brother, and my mom. This was the fun brother. He had all the cool friends, played the best music, and he could cook too. Life was still good.

Then one day, my mom announced we were moving back to the Midwest. I was devastated! Now I understood how my siblings felt when we moved to New Jersey. However, moving was not the only crushing part of the story. The reason we were moving was that my grandmother had grown ill with lung cancer. My mom did a lot of traveling back and forth to get things set up. My grandmother was very independent and did not want to live with anyone. My mom bought her another house in E. St. Louis and bought us a house in St. Louis, MO. Unfortunately, before we could all move into our new homes, my grandmother passed away in the hospital. Since our old house was sold, the new house was already bought, and my mom had transferred. The move to St. Louis, MO, was unavoidable.

CHAPTER 2

The New Kid

While my brother was tying up all the loose ends with the move in New Jersey for my mom, we relocated to another great neighborhood with a park at the end of the block. The area we lived in was called University City. This was a middle-class suburbs area in St. Louis, right outside of St. Louis city. There were kids in the neighborhood but not as many as my old one. They did not seem to play outside as much as where I used to live. Maybe the difference was we were older. I was turning 11 years old and starting middle school in the fall. I did not realize my childhood as I knew it was over.

My dad was moving with us. He was retired Navy, and for many years I thought my dad was always my dad. In my mind, he was in the military, which would explain why 3 of my siblings entered the military. I later learned that was not the case. My parents met on one of those business trips when we were living up north and they fell in love. He was there for my mom when she had to travel for my grandmother. When we moved to the Midwest, everyone moved together, me, my mom, my brother and now, my dad. I was happy about it. We all loved him, and Mom seemed more at peace when he was there.

When I started 6th grade, I met a lot of new kids, but the biggest difference between University City, the city residents fondly nicknamed " U-City," and Landing, was there were a lot more kids that looked like me in U-City. Our neighborhood was more mixed which I was comfortable with. Unfortunately, that is where the similarities ended. I found the kids topic of conversation a little strange. They knew about stuff I later learned only adults should know. Before I moved, I was still playing tag and making mud pies. These kids had no interest in that. They seemed a lot older than me. They reminded me of my siblings. Much of what I heard; I did not understand. I felt like an outsider and not as intelligent as everyone else. I could not understand how they knew this stuff at our age. That year I met a guy who went on to become one of my best friends. When he realized how naive I was, he protected me like I was his little sister. I remember a time at lunch when I first heard the term "bust a nut," and I turned to my best friend and asked him what did that mean? He immediately snapped and said, "Don't use that type of language around her! She doesn't know about that stuff!" I was a little embarrassed about him exposing that I was not up to date on what everyone seemed to know about but me, however, I was happy he was there to help shield me as much as he could. Unfortunately, from there, it all went downhill. After sixth grade, he moved to another part of the city. As much as he tried, he could not protect me from all the stuff I would hear and witness.

I may have been introduced to inappropriate language, but I had a strong religious family that kept me grounded in faith. My family still had no church home, but we had bible studies a few times per week. My parents and I would sit in the living room, discussing selected chapters and verses. I had my children's bible, but I was able to follow along. My family was so strong in their faith that, if Jehovah Witnesses came to our home, my mother would welcome them in for a deep discussion about the Lord. At times all the bible study discussions would become overwhelming, but it kept me grounded from falling into the lifestyle many of my classmates were living.

Sixth grade was quite an experience and a contrast to what I was accustomed to hearing and seeing. I thought I had a grasp on things by the end of that school year, but I soon realized that was only the beginning. In the seventh grade, I was still singing in the chorus and still innocent. That year, our choir took an overnight trip to Branson, MO, to perform. Our group was assigned to 4 girls per room. For one night, some of the girls I was assigned to room with planned to have visitors when our chaperones went to sleep. I remember late at night; one of the girls who was my friend, woke me up saying we were about to have company. She always looked out for me, and she knew I did not understand what was about to happen. Our room had two full size beds and across the room were 2 comfortable oversized chairs. I sat in one of the chairs with a pillow and a blanket. I watched the girls get ready, and when we got the knock on the door, they answered it to 4 guys coming in. My friend told the 4th guy, "Not her. You need to go to another room." The other three paired off and got in bed. The lights were off, and I could not really see much, but I heard a lot of noises. I was a little uncomfortable with what I heard and afraid we would get in trouble. I may not have done anything, but I knew those boys should not have been there. I slept in the chair that night, even after the boys left.

I knew I was not allowed to have any guy friends like that, and I knew what I witnessed in Branson was against the teachings in the bible. Someone told on the kids who snuck into different rooms, and we were all questioned. I just told them I slept all night, so I did not witness any visitors. I knew it was not right to lie, but I did not want to get my friends in trouble. Besides, I knew if my parents found out I would not be in chorus any longer.

In seventh grade, I had not had my first boyfriend yet, but there were boys that liked me. The most that happened with me was a boy holding my hand or walking me home. I had never even been kissed. I heard so many stories about what my classmates were doing, and I could not imagine doing any of that until I was married. I was kind of embarrassed to be the "good girl." The one who did not understand half of what they were saying or doing. I would just sit and listen, feeling like I needed to take notes so I could remember to ask questions later. It felt like I was the only one who studied the bible. They did not seem to care about sins or going against the teachings on fornication. I was also surprised at the freedom these girls had. My parents were strict. They knew my every move. Some of these girls had so much freedom, maybe too much. They were having babies and I barely understood how babies were made! Even with having four older siblings, I never heard or saw anything I should not. It was moments like this I wish I could climb up a dirt hill or go make mud pies. With all this new exposure, I knew my life would never be the same again.

After such an intense school year, I was happy to have some neighborhood friends to hang out with over the summer. Some were a little older but nice and easy to talk to. They did not go to the public schools, and they did not look like me. It may be strange to say, but I was comfortable with that. I really enjoyed their company. I could talk to these girls about some of the things that happened at school, and they would answer all my questions. They were a little surprised by what was going on but were more concerned about me. They would also encourage me to stay on my path of church, and that gave me peace.

That summer, I had a birthday party before returning to school. I was turning 13 years old. My mom set everything up in the backyard, and there were purple decorations everywhere. All the kids from the neighborhood came. We played games and ate. It felt like I was back in New Jersey. My mom brought one of my gifts from the garage. My dad had bought me a red bike, and I was so excited. It had the water bottle and everything on it almost identical to his. He was an avid bike rider, and I wanted one just like his. It was the best gift ever. He was on a business trip, so he did not get to see my reaction, but just when I was taking my bow off to ride it with my friends, there was someone there to see my reaction.

My mom called me over to meet someone. She introduced him as my dad. I thought it was a joke and I laughed. I remember saying, "You're not my dad. My dad is on a business trip. My dad bought me this bike." My mom said to him, I will explain it to her later. She told me to go play with my friends. I never saw that man again. Later that evening, my mom explained to me who he was and gave me the only two pictures she had of him. I kind of looked like him, but I looked like my dad too. It did not matter. There was only one dad to me.

— CHAPTER 3 —

Never The Same

My eighth-grade year was pretty much the same as the ones before. I hung out with the same friends, and I listened to the same types of stories. Their lives had not changed, and neither had mine. As I got to know some of the other quiet girls, I realized I was not the only one who was inexperienced. They were just listening as girls told their stories, just like I was. It felt good to know I was not some foreign being. There were others and more importantly, there were others who knew the bible too.

Since I had friendships that lasted over the years, I was able to visit a couple of people at their home. One friend came from a household stricter than mine! It was just her and her mom and they were deep into the church. I liked hanging out with her. We seemed to click right away. One day I was over at her house, and her cousin came by to visit. He was older and extremely popular. He went to the high school and everyone knew him for closely resembling the singer Prince. He was also the captain of the wrestling team. So, imagine my surprise when he showed interest in me, a middle schooler! I was so shy I could barely talk. I had never really talked to a boy before, well, not romantically. The boys I knew were silly and gross. He seemed nice, and he was not bothered by the fact that I did not know a lot of things like he did. He said we could be friends and asked for my number. Since it was not a romantic thing, I figured it would be okay. I mean, he was a relative of one of my closest friends. How bad could he be?

We talked occasionally, not every day. One day he asked me if he could walk me home after school. He said he would be out of school by the time my bus dropped me at the bus stop, and I told him that would be okay. He met me at the bus stop as promised. Everyone on the bus was totally shocked he was there for me. I was so nervous that he wanted to walk me home and I thought it was sweet. We cut through the park and walked down the block to my house. We talked on the porch for a minute. I could not have company. Plus, my brother was home, and he would not like a guy hanging around. I was about to go inside when he asked if he could use the bathroom. Since we had a half bath right down the hall near the kitchen, I thought it would be okay. I let him in and showed him where the bathroom was. The basement door was near the bathroom and that is where my brother's room was. I explained to him if he heard the door, it was my brother. As he went to the bathroom, I ran upstairs to put my books down. When I went back in the hallway to go back downstairs, he was upstairs. I panicked and told him he could not come up here. He ignored me and said this was a nice house, looking around. I stood there frozen, telling him he had to go before I got in trouble. He kept checking out the house, walking further down the hall. I grabbed his arm and tried to pull him back the other way when he grabbed me and spun me into the family room. I fell over the arm of the couch onto the floor, between the coffee table and the couch. He fell on top of me, and I kept telling him to get up. He was super strong and heavy. He pinned my arms down and used his body to pin the rest of me. With his other hand, he yanked my jeans and underwear down. I cried out for my brother, but he put his hand over my mouth. I kept trying to scream and wiggle free, but it did not work. What I was doing was making it easier for him to access me. He forced himself into me as I laid under him crying. It did not take long for him to finish, and he hopped up, fixed himself, and said he would call me later as he left. I was on the floor in pain, trying to make sense of what just happened.

Had I just had sex? What will happen now? Am I going to go to hell? Is God mad at me? Why am I in so much pain? Why didn't my brother come help me? I cannot tell my parents. Now I am one of those girls at my school. I tried to clean up, and I went to bed early, not sure what to do. At school the next day, I had gym with my friend who protected me last year at Branson. We were sitting on the mats, and I told her, "I think I had sex yesterday." She stopped and looked at me, asking, "With who?" She knew I had no boyfriend. I told her everything. I was shaking uncontrollably. I told her, "If that is sex, I don't like it." She said, "Sweetie look at me. That was not sex. You were raped." I said, "Raped? How? I know him and some of his family." She said, "That is date rape." I had never heard of that. I thought rape was only by strangers who snatched women and girls off the streets. She explained everything to me. I cried and cried. What was I supposed to do now? Raped? Rape was a really bad thing. That is a crime.

I went through the rest of my day in shock. When I got home, I called his home until someone answered. His mother. She could tell something was wrong. She told him to pick up the phone, and as soon as he got the phone, he thought she had hung up her line, but she had not. I screamed, "You raped me!" He was caught off guard, and before he could say anything, his mother said, "WHAT?! Is this true?" He said, "No, momma! She is lying! She wanted it!" I said, "You liar! I was a virgin! I didn't want anything from you!" His mother asked him, "Did you wear a condom?" And he responded, "Yes!" I screamed, "You are a liar again! You did not wear a condom! You held me down and snatched my clothes off! You never put on a condom!" His mother made him come into the room with her. She kept the line open, but I heard her whispering to him in angry tones before the line went dead.

I was crying and shaking. I felt horrible and sick for the rest of the night. I must have been crying loud enough for my mom to hear because she came into my room, left the lights off and sat on my bed. I told her everything that happened, and she cried too. Afterwards, she said we cannot tell your father or your brother. They will kill him. We never spoke about it again.

— CHAPTER 4 —

Confusion, Guilt and Anger

Nothing happened. Nothing. I was attacked by someone I thought was a good person and there were no consequences. I thought when people did bad things like this, they went to jail. If my mother will not allow me to talk about it, how will he go to jail? Why won't she let us do anything? We did not talk about it. We did not pray about it. Nothing else was mentioned from that moment to this one. Is it because God said vengeance is mine? If that is true, why hasn't He done anything? Maybe He is too mad at me. Maybe his vengeance is on me, not him. Maybe I was the bad one, the disobedient one. I was not supposed to have anyone in the house, and I did not listen. This is my fault and God is mad at me.

My 13-year-old mind did not have the full understanding of how God worked. I was a child from a strict religious household who retained bits and pieces of my Bible lessons. I believed I was damaged, tainted and God was not happy with me. My confusion and guilt kept me from continuing my bible studies. Since my mother knew what happened, she did not push me, which was surprising. It only allowed me to withdraw more into myself and stay in my room. I was depressed for a long time. I felt guilty and did not know how to make it up to God. I studied hard in school and graduated from the 8th grade with A's and B's, but the only thing that came out of that was my parents bought me a small personal Bible as my graduation gift to keep with me always.

My little bit of happiness came from graduating with my friends, that was fun. However, leaving eighth grade meant going to the high school where he was. What if I saw him? How would I react? Would he feel guilty and go the opposite way? Or would he try to embarrass me in front of everyone? I felt sick all summer every time I thought about it. I have heard rumors about high school students and how they treat freshmen. All I need is for him to make me look like an awful person after what he did to me.

I dropped out of all activities outside of chorus. My Mom did not understand why I was no longer interested in running track since I did well in my races. I never told her that I did not want to wear anything that brought attention to my body. I did not think she would understand how uncomfortable I was. In the chorus I could blend in. No one was looking at me, and I was comfortable with that. I wore baggy clothes so no one could see my body. It seemed like that was all boys wanted to do, and it made me uncomfortable. Then it got to the point where dressing that way, did not hide everything. It seemed to make the boys want to look harder. At this point, I was angry because it seemed like no matter what I did, their behavior would not change.

During my freshman year, I did not see my attacker at all, and I was grateful for that. One day, I was walking down the hallway when I saw four guys leaning up against the lockers between classes. They were upperclassmen. They were well dressed, and you could tell they were well known in the school. They were looking and commenting on every girl that passed them. I was not comfortable passing by them, and I wish I were invisible at that moment. As I passed by, they got quiet for a moment, before one called me fresh meat. Ignoring the comment was the easy part, but right when I passed by the last guy, he smacked me on my butt hard. I stopped and turned around when another guy yelled out, "what is your problem?!" I stared hard at the one that hit me and remembered his face. When I turned to walk away, they all laughed and made more rude comments. I later caught him in the hall solo and pushed him hard against the locker. When he turned to face me, I grabbed him between his legs and squeezed with every ounce of strength my anger could muster and told him he better not ever touch me again. Staring at him in his eyes, his eyes filled with tears, he nodded his head in agreement, and I never had another problem out of him or any of his friends again.

My anger ended up taking over a few months into my freshmen year, and I had a chip on my shoulder. I had a smart mouth and was ready to fight anyone who looked like they wanted to touch me. For my first year and a half of high school, I was in a lot of fistfights with boys. I fought like my life depended on it. I would not let another boy touch me like that again. I hated them. They were evil, and I wanted them all dead. I only had love for my brothers and my dad. I did have a few guy friends, but none of them looked at me the wrong way. I was more damaged than I realized.

I skipped school a lot. I would spend the day at the park or just walking around. My focus was lost. I had no dreams. I did not want to be a part of anything. I did not want to be here. What was the point? God was mad at me. I was damaged goods. Something must be wrong with me because boys had no respect for me. It was not long before boys disrespected friends of mine. So, one by one, I would find them and threaten or fight them too.

One morning before school, a friend of mine was walking in the building, and as she passed by a group of guys hanging out on the front stairs, one of the guys yelled, "No you can't suck my dick!" Everyone on the stairs looked at her because he said her name. This young lady was the sweetest person you would ever want to meet. Incredibly quiet and well mannered.

When she came running up to me at my locker in tears, explaining what just happened, I snapped. I skipped several classes until I found him during a class change. I slammed him up again the lockers off his feet and screamed in his face several obscenities and threats. He tried the same tactic on me he had on her, but I came right back with a nastier response. The embarrassment fell on him. I told him he will apologize to her or much worse will happen. A teacher pulled me off him. Later that day, my friend told me he apologized for making a joke at her expense.

I had knives, razors and any other weapons I could get my hands on. I wanted these disrespectful guys to know they could do nothing to hurt me, and I was willing to end them if I had to. That scared many of them. A lot apologized and other people thought I was crazy. I knew many people, had a few friends but I hung out with no one. I wanted to be alone. I had given up on life at this point. I was willing to risk it all by taking my anger and frustration out on every guy that did not know what manners were. I was tired of seeing guys treat females like something they could play with at their leisure without consequence.

Even though this had become a way of life that kept me sane, I had no idea that, yet again, life was going to change. Since the eighth grade, I kept running into this guy from around the neighborhood. Our paths crossed a few times due to our friends dating or just hanging in the same places. The chip on my shoulder was firmly in place, so for me being anything more than friends, if that, was not going to happen. Regardless, he was always respectful, which made him stand out to me. When we had a class together, that is when everything changed, and I got to know my soon to be first boyfriend.

CHAPTER 5

The Haven

The only men in my life I ever trusted were my father and my brothers. They were the only ones I felt safe with, which is what made this guy so different. He never gave me a weird feeling in his presence. He was always polite, and I felt a sense of comfort when he was around.

A year back, I hung out in an area called The Loop. The Loop was like a "downtown" U. City. There were tons of shops, restaurants and markets. It was a nice strip to walk and plenty of kids hung out there. What I liked about it was that it was a mixture of all types, from Goth to Preppy and everything in between. This is where our then best friends met, exchanged numbers and saw each other. Dating was the last thing on my mind, so I always played the background. I was not sociable; I was just there. I noticed him, but I did not pay a lot of attention to any guy back then. Of course, at that age, relationships were short-lived, so our friends dating did not last long. Hence me running into him off and on.

I remember walking to school the beginning of my sophomore year and seeing him with his same group of friends from middle school. I had not seen them walk this way before. It was strange but I felt kind of relieved when I saw him. I spoke to him as if I did it all the time. He looked at me strangely like, "why are you speaking to me?" But in true gentlemanly fashion, he spoke back. I fell into step with him and started a little small talk that morning. He obliged me, but I am sure he was thinking, "what's her deal?" Later that day, we discovered we had a class together, and I sat behind him. I could not explain it, but I was drawn to him, and that was the beginning of us.

He was nice and funny. He did not look at me like I was something to use and toss away. He treated me like a real friend. He did not try anything out of the way, and I felt respected around him. Our friendship grew to more, and he started to melt the ice from my heart. I learned to trust him. I felt completely safe around him. I was not fighting anymore. I was not as angry as I used to be, but the biggest thing I noticed was that, if he was by my side, I was not disrespected. People recognized us as a couple. I had to talk to my parents about having a boyfriend. They agreed and wanted to meet him.

The Saturday he met my parents was almost like running into a good cop bad cop situation. My mom was nice, and my dad was too but in a dad way. My father was licensed to buy and sell firearms. He went to the range every Saturday morning, so by the time I brought my soon-to-be-boyfriend to the house to meet them, Daddy was just getting home, sitting in his office about to clean all the guns he used that day. When I introduced him to my father, we both kind of froze, looking at the spread Daddy had just laid out on the table. My father had him take a seat across the table from him so they could "talk." I was freaking out and ran and told my mom what Daddy was doing. She laughed and said, "he'll be fine." I was on pins and needles because I did not want Daddy to run him off. However, this guy never failed me. He may have been super nervous and thought my family was crazy, but he saw it through and still wanted to date me. He earned my parent's respect, and he became my first official boyfriend.

We dated through the rest of my high school years. We attended my Junior prom and our Junior/ Senior prom. We planned for our future. We wanted to go off to school together, and he even had blueprints for designing our first home. He was a dreamer, and I loved that about him. It took me from the harsh realities I had been dealing with and gave me something to look forward to. He may not have come from money, but he dreamed like we would have a million dollars in the bank, and I believed him too. He showed me parts of the city I had never seen before. We did not just catch the bus around the city, some nights he would rent a limousine and take me on real dates. Riding around the city at night was a different feeling. All the beautiful lights were very romantic. He would cook dinners and he even played my secret admirer, leaving anonymous notes in my locker. He always kept it fun with roses and gifts. His thoughtfulness reminded me of how my father was with my mother.

Everyone at school believed we would be married. They wrote in my memory book about us, and it made me feel good to know this was real. Unfortunately, every happy story does not end that way. During our time together, He and some of his friends formed a musical group and started performing. They used to sing and dance and were good. They toured and put on a few local shows. At first, they were only known for their dancing skills, so to add vocals was a big surprise. The first time I got to see them perform on stage at one of their shows, it was short lived because I was rushed out the back door by security. Some of the group's fans got angry after discovering I was a girlfriend of one of the members. I only got to see him perform that one time after that we agreed it was not a safe environment for me.

He had to practice a lot, and I picked up my first job at the local pizza restaurant. If I had free time and he was busy, I would hang out with friends and vice versa. Being apart was new and different for us, but he was pursuing one of his passions, which of course, I supported. After our Junior/Senior prom, things took a turn for the worse. The summer after prom I was at home sleeping when I received a late phone call from my cousin. She was hanging out at home with this guy she was dating and showed him our prom picture. He claimed to recognize my boyfriend because he was also dating his cousin. For anyone to try and tell me my boyfriend was cheating on me was something I would never believe. There were so many people trying to tear us apart and my cousin and I were not as close as we used to be. To prove what she was saying, she put her friend on the phone. He told me his family had plans to go to Six Flags, and my boyfriend was going too. I still did not believe it. I did not know this guy, and I was not going to trust his word. So, he came up with an idea to call him and play as if he was doing a final headcount for the Six Flags outing. I agreed. We called him, and when I heard my boyfriend say he was not going, I lost it. I went off. I was so angry I was shaking. When he realized I was on the phone, he was shocked and then said he could explain. It was late at night, and I had to sneak out of the house to meet him. In my anger, I was not thinking straight. I went to the basement and took one of my father's small handguns and tucked it under my sweatshirt.

I felt numb walking up the street to meet him. I felt nothing but disappointment when I saw him. How could he do this to me? To us? After all these years? He approached me slowly, trying to explain that she was an ex-girlfriend of his, and they never had closure. The more he spoke, the angrier I became. We were standing under a streetlight, and I remember reaching behind me for the gun while he was apologizing. I looked up at the time to see an officer slow rolling past us. I did not pull out the gun, but I heard him say he would make it right and tell her about us. The next day he set everything up for us to speak to her together and clear all of this up.

When we met up to go to her house, I realized two things, the mood was awkward between us, and there were several people following us. I do not know how so many people discovered what was going on, but by the time we reached her home, there were people all up and down the block, waiting to see what would happen. My cousin was there, and so was his ex-girlfriend's relative. Her mother let us in, and we waited in the living room. I was still angry and hurt, and he looked very regretful. When she finally came downstairs, I snapped off, "This is her?! You cheated on me for her?! She isn't even cute!" Yes, super rude, I know, but I was hot as fire. He dropped his head in embarrassment, and her mom walked out of the kitchen, staring hard at me. He took over the conversation and explained to her how this all happened. He explained to her when she moved, he thought it was over and was surprised she came home thinking they were still together. He initially met up with her to tell her he moved on and to get closure, but he did not know how. He explained, we had been together for a couple of years, and I was who he wanted to be with. When he said this, she tried to snap off claiming I did not love him, she did and how they never broke up. She was very emotional and yelling. She was hurt but not crazy. She remained standing behind the couch near the stairs. I may not have been fighting anymore, but that part of me was still ready. He shut her down by saying it was over between them and he was with me. When he was done, we got up to walk out. The only thing I said to her before I left was to keep my name out of her mouth because she does not know me. The crowd was still outside. People love drama. We walked home, but home for us would never be the same.

The trust was broken. We went through the motions of spending time together, walking to school, doing homework, but honestly, I did not feel the same way. I was hurt in a new way I did not understand. I knew what caused it, but I did not know how to fix it. I felt cold towards him. He tried to get things back on track, but I did not believe anything he told me. He had lied to me for a while to cover that situation, so in my eyes, everything was a lie. We started going through these little breakups. We argued a lot, and nothing felt right.

One of the Washington University campuses was near the pizza place where I worked. A lot of college kids frequented there talking about the various parties and they often left flyers. I decided to go to one since I would be in college soon. I wanted to have fun. It seemed like fun stopped for me when our relationship started falling apart. I told him about the party. Even though we hung out earlier in the day, we went to the party separately with friends. Being at the party I felt a sense of freedom. I did not feel so heavy and I missed having that feeling. I knew going to college was a few months away and I was ready for a change. When I saw my boyfriend, I realized at that moment we had to stop going through this. Neither one of us was happy. As hard as he tried to make us work, I was broken. I loved him but I did not know how to come back from what we had been through. I decided to end our relationship. The way things had been going for us, I felt it was time to move on. I pulled him outside the party and told him how I felt. It was harsh because I was speaking from a place of pain instead of the love, I still had for him. When I looked in his eyes, I saw regret for what he had done, hurt from what I had caused and the love that he still had for me. I wanted to love him back, but it seemed like I could only lash out my hurt unto him. After I broke up with him, I went back to the party and tried to leave everything on the dance floor. I was convinced that if my first love, my first everything could hurt me after all we shared, there were not any good guys out there.

CHAPTER 6

College

College life was different for me. It was the first time I encountered people from different areas throughout St. Louis regularly. Normally, whatever I did was mostly within the boundaries of the area I lived in. Occasionally I would venture out to new places if my parents were driving or if I caught the bus downtown to the mall.

Meeting people from various parts of the city was fun because I hung out with people I may have never met. All the different personalities, styles of dress and dance was like a whole new world. I felt like I could spread my wings a little. I cut my hair and got a little more comfortable in my skin. I was not wearing revealing clothes, but I was wearing clothes that fit me. I walked with a little more confidence than I felt. I smiled and was more outspoken than I had been in high school. I refused to go back to being angry all the time. Although I was in the same city, I was not with the same people, and I was not the same either.

I dated a guy for a short time who worked at the same pizza place as I did. It seemed exciting to have a guy with his own car. We would take drives around town and had more freedom to get to other parts of the city. I was spellbound by the differences, not so much by the guy. Shortly after we started dating, he became very possessive and controlling. This is when the rose-colored glasses had come off. If I were doing something he did not like or approved of, he would verbally tear me down and make me feel less than. Even if I were trying to set a goal and work towards it, he would try to discourage me and tell me I was not smart enough or I was reaching too far. He was a slight bit older than me, so at first, I trusted his word on a lot of things. As time went on, I realized he was not speaking from a place of knowledge but instead from his insecurities. When he met me, I was in my senior year of high school, and he knew I did not know much about the city or have much life experience. However, when I started at the local community college, I met people. I started learning more and wanting to explore. The minute I tried to spread my wings, it felt like they were clipped.

I remember thinking I would try to transfer to a school in Atlanta like Clark Atlanta University or Spellman since my brother-in-law had attended Morehouse. It was also a plus that my sister lived there. She helped me pick the schools. I loved when my parents and I would take road trips every year to see her. I planned on going down to see the colleges on my spring break. Initially, it was just me going to Atlanta. When he learned about this, he decided to make it a road trip for the both of us. That was interesting for me since it was the first time I had traveled with a guy. He had a cousin who lived there. I was planning to stay with my sister while I was there, but since he would not be able to stay there too, he insisted we both stay with his cousin. His cousin was nice, and her apartment was kind of small, but we made it work. I got a chance to see my sister and the colleges. I felt bad for not staying with her and not allowing my family to take me on the college tours. It was a little crazy downtown since it was also Freak Nik weekend. This is when the students from historically black colleges got together in Atlanta on their spring break to party. At Piedmont park there would be big performances from the hottest artists, students riding up and down the street and partying where they stood. I had never seen anything like this before, and it was overwhelming. My sister later explained that what I saw was not the norm. Most of the people there were out of towners, and it would not be that way if I decided to attend the schools. I was excited about the schools, and I could not wait to put in my applications. I noticed the more I spoke about the schools, the more irritated he became.

Once we were back in St. Louis, I was at his house filling out the applications when I asked his opinion on what I should write my essay on for Spellman? I was nervous, and I wanted to make a good impression. He laughed and said, "Do you really think you would get in? You need to shoot lower for Clark Atlanta University, and they probably won't take you either." I was really hurt. I told him, "I may have struggled in high school for personal reasons, but since I've been at the community college, I've been on the Dean's list. He said, "You need more than book smarts, and being a sheltered daddy's girl won't get you in." I knew I had not been in any extracurricular activities since my sophomore year of high school, and I would need something more than simply great grades. I had no community service experience, and I started to think maybe he was right. Maybe I was not good enough to get into these schools. What was I going to do with my life?

I got down on myself and my grades reflected that. I hung out more in the game room after class than I did studying. My life was taking a turn for the worst. We took a trip to his grandmother's house in Carlyle, IL for a family get together. It was about an hour and a half away. He was on another nasty rampage. Once we got there, you could cut the tension with a knife. His grandmother watched our interactions and once he left to go fishing with his uncle at the lake, she asked me if he was abusing me. I told her no and she said if he has not, he will. "He has that same look in his eyes his daddy uses to have." That scared me, a lot. His tone was getting nastier, but he never acted like he wanted to hit me. His grandmother told me the story of his mother and father. His father abused his mother before, during and after the pregnancy. His father used to drink a lot and once he was drunk, he would be physically abusive to his mother. Even having their baby in her arms did not stop him from hitting her. Her brothers used to fight him, but it never stopped him from coming for her. His grandmother told his mother, " you are the only one who can stop him from abusing you." His mother joined the police academy. Since his father was drunk all the time, he slept a lot. During those hours, she was training to be an officer. The day she graduated, she came home, and he had been drinking. He came for her and she threw her badge on the table and asked him, "Do you know what will happen to you for assaulting a police officer?" She was able to throw him out of her house and keep him out. I was shaken by the story, but I felt empowered as well.

I was still struggling in school and trying to decide about my life when my parents announced that Daddy's job was relocating to Virginia. My mom explained that she had someone who could help me get into Howard University. I knew nothing about the school. I was upset and explained that my life was here, in St. Louis. I did not want to move. While this was going on, I wanted to end this relationship I was in. I was not feeling it and I had so much to think about. My head was not on straight, I was spiraling but I stuck with my decision.

Ending that relationship was hard. Not because I was emotionally caught up, because he was determined to keep it going. The little stuff I had of his, I packed in a bag and sat it outside for him to pick up. We had been in an argument and told him I wanted this relationship to be over. He came by that night to pick up the bag from the porch, but when he did not see me, he left it and kept calling me. I finally answered. He was full of apologies and he wanted to talk. When I went downstairs, he came on the porch, grabbed me by my neck, dug his nails in my throat and picked me up off my feet. He had been drinking. He said, "This relationship isn't over until I say it's over, bitch!" He slammed my back against the brick house and then yanked me into the bushes where the branches scratched me and back against the house. I was kicking and swinging, trying to breathe. Tears ran down my face as I fought to get loose. He said other words, but I could not hear him. I was trying to live. Our house was in a gated community that was patrolled at night. I just knew any moment an officer would roll up, but one never came. When he let me go, I fell against the door. I looked at him, ran inside, locking the door. I kept hearing his grandmother's voice saying that if he is not abusing you now, he will.

The next day I had purple and blue bruises down my back and his finger and nail prints on my neck. I had scratches from the bushes. I cried in the shower from the sting of the cuts and the pain in my body. I covered up so my parents would not see. I knew they would call the police, take legal action, and I would be on the way to Virginia. Luckily, it was cold, so I wore a turtleneck. When I got to school, I pulled friends in the bathroom to show them what happened. Some of my guy friends were ready to end him, but I could not have that on my conscience. When it was time to go home, I saw him driving around the campus where I would catch the bus. He knew my schedule. I was scared to leave the school. I watched him from the window circling around and wondering how I would get home. Friends gave me rides home every day for a while to avoid him.

My parents gave me the okay to remain in St. Louis. My mom planned with my oldest brother to get an apartment for us and they would pay my half. Moving day came and the apartment I moved into with my oldest brother was not as luxurious as my parent's home, but it allowed me to stay. It was not the best decision. My grades tanked. I missed my parents and although I had a new level of freedom, this move only brought more drama in my life.

I did not want another relationship. It had been a few months since I had gotten rid of my crazy ex. Avoiding him worked. I went on dates here and there, but it did not take long to see that a little crazy was everywhere. I went on a date with a guy who believed in disciplining your woman the way you do your children. Then there was the date-you-when-it's-convenient guy, then there was the emotional guy, who got mad and did not speak to you for days but showed up later like it is all good. It was exhausting and I was over it. I was trying to focus on passing that spring semester, when I got a surprise visit from my crazy ex. How he found me, I do not know how. I think he had to follow me from work and noticed that I was taking a different way home. Although he no longer worked there, I still worked at the same place, so maybe it was not so hard to find me. I had one of those stupid doors where you could not tell who was there. When I answered, he pushed his way in, cursing and calling me every name but a child of

God. He ran up in my home like he had the right to look for someone. I ran up the stairs behind him, telling him to get out. He got in my face. He had been drinking again. I backed up. I said, "you may have caught me off guard the first time, but there won't be a second." He pushed and I pushed back. He swung. I swung. We kept going. I hit him with everything I had and everything I found. He threatened to kill me and anyone he found with me. He left. My brother was never home. I knew my ex had a gun. I started to call the police and then I remembered, his mother was the police. I called her. I told her everything and that I knew he had a gun in her house. I told her where I remembered him keeping it. She said I should have called her when he first touched me. She told me not to worry, that she would get him when he walked in. I never heard from him again. How did I not see the signs?

CHAPTER 7

Trying Again

After I knew for sure my crazy ex was out of my life, I decided to try and focus on getting my life together. My grades were in the toilet and I knew I would have to make better decisions. Being separated from my parents left an emptiness and loneliness I was not expecting. I was still in touch with a few friends from middle and high school. It was nice to hang out and catch up with people that knew me. People I already established friendships with. Friends I could talk to.

Just about everyone had gone off to college, which made it harder to keep in touch. I contacted a girl friend of mine I had known since middle school. Summer break had just started, and it was a lot easier to hang out. She told me her cousin was home from school and we should go see him. I had known her cousin since middle school. I met him through the boy from 6th grade who protected me like his sister. I did not see him often since he lived in a different part of the city unless I went to the mall because he worked at Mrs. Field's Cookies in the Galleria Mall when we were in high school. He was always flirty, but I always had a boyfriend when he showed interest. Most of the time I did not take him seriously. He was dating someone in high school too. Plus, he was a football player at his high school, which means he had girls around him regularly.

The great thing about him was that he was a good listener. Before my first boyfriend, we all used to sit on 3-way calling and talk for hours. It was fun. Occasionally we would talk about my head bumps with my mom or problems I had at school. He gave me good advice, and he was good at calming me down when I was angry. We developed a good friendship and he was someone I could trust.

The three of us hung out that summer and it was fun and relaxing. By the end of that summer, we had grown closer and gave dating a try. It was difficult for us because we went to college in two different states. He went to school in Mississippi. When I was packing to visit him for homecoming weekend, my high school sweetheart stopped by. I must have been the easiest person to find. He had joined the Navy like my dad and told me he was getting married. Although I had moved on, it was a major blow. I just started this relationship and he had asked someone to marry him! It was strange to picture him having a life with someone else. That was supposed to be us. I thought about when I tried to get him back shortly after our breakup, but he did not want to be with me anymore. I had to respect where we were in life now. I walked around packing for my trip as if his news had no effect on me. I told him congratulations, but I kept moving so he could not read my face. I still loved him, and I probably always would. He was my first love. Now that the dust had settled, there was just soreness where the pain was. Before he left, he gave me a picture of himself from bootcamp that I kept under my pillow for a while. Our moment together was awkward. How could I still be in love with him? How was it that his life was moving along so smoothly? I had not been the same without him, but I could not say any of this. It was also out of my hands and I was not in the business of breaking up happy homes. Besides, I had a boyfriend I needed to focus on.

Although I was in college, my co-worker who was like a big brother chaperoned my visit. I talked to him about everything since I felt alone in the city with my parents gone. He drove me down to Mississippi for the weekend and got our hotel rooms set up. He had family there, so he hung out with them. I knew he was only a phone call away if I needed anything. Being in Mississippi was different. The students seemed nice, but several locals I ran into seemed racist. My boyfriend and I went to a convenience store and after I paid for my stuff, the cashier tossed my change on the counter. I was outraged and went off. My boyfriend pulled me out of the store, trying to get me to let it go. I had only seen behavior like that in the movies. Outside of that incident, I had fun touring the school and attending the homecoming activities. However, I was feeling uneasy the whole time. During the step show, it felt like I was having an anxiety attack. One fraternity had smoke in their routine, and I remember feeling as though I could not breathe. I tried to leave the bleachers and head out of the gym for fresh air, but I did not make it outside before I passed out. I must have been unconscious for only a moment because my boyfriend and one of his childhood friends helped me outside for some fresh air and then to the car so I could go back to my hotel. Apparently, receiving that news of my ex getting married affected me more than I realized. I could not stop thinking about it the entire weekend.

Although it was nice to get out of town and experience a University's homecoming, I felt somewhat out of place. He seemed happy there with his friends and fraternity brothers. It brought home the understanding of how lost I felt. My grades were in the toilet, I felt like I had no support and I had no direction. I kept thinking when was the last time I laughed and had fun like those students? When I returned to St. Louis, I felt alone and depressed. I had friends I spoke to here and there. I hung out with people occasionally at college, but there was not anyone that I was close with. The guy I dated through high school was my closest friend. Prior to him, I stayed more to myself. I had girlfriends I was cool with but no one I spoke to regularly. I was truly alone. I tried writing to my boyfriend more, but the response was minimal if I heard anything back at all. He came home when he could. His older car always gave him trouble. When he finally did come home, it was not until the holiday break. We fought a lot and even though we were trying to make the long-distance thing work. It did not. We were much better as friends, plain and simple. It is unfortunate we did not realize that prior to me getting pregnant.

I moved into my own place on the southside of St. Louis. Since I was in school, my parents paid for half of my rent and utilities. My pregnancy was rough on me mentally and physically. I had some complications and was put on bed rest, which caused me to have to drop out of school. I was alone in the city and knew nothing about having a baby. I was afraid but I had to mentally prepare myself. I talked to God a lot which I had not done in a long time. When I was back on my feet, I found a new job and worked full time. I started planning for my baby to come. I purchased everything I could think of to buy.

My baby's father came home periodically from school to check on us. It was not easy to go back to being how we were before we dated since we had a baby on the way. We were in two different worlds now. He was in school, having fun with his friends and I was working full time preparing for a baby. It was awkward when he came home for the summer because the baby was due in August. He wanted to help me prepare but finding a job was not easy for him. He eventually found work he hated, and it kept him in a bad mood. We bumped heads a lot, but he still came around to make sure I was okay. During one of our rough times, I was headed to work and forgot some of the downtown streets were blocked due to the Fourth of July holiday celebrations. I was catching the bus and had to walk much further than usual in high ninety-degree weather while I was 8 months pregnant. I had water with me, but it was not enough. By the time I reached my job, I was having abdominal pains and breathing hard. Security called an ambulance and I went directly to the ER. The hospital called his aunt's house to let him know I was in the hospital. When he did show up, he had his cousin and his cousin's friend with him. He asked the doctor if I was about to have the baby. The doctor told him no, I was dehydrated and having Braxton Hicks pains, also known as false labor pains. After I rested and was hydrated enough, I could go home. He turned to me and said, call me if you need a ride and left the hospital. I was hurt because I was laying in the hospital with his child and he knew I did not have a car. I would not allow that to break me. I had the hospital call me a cab home.

We did not speak for a while and when we did, I was different towards him. We had decent days, but I did not see him the same. He would bring me food when he came by and I had gone to a movie once with him and his cousin. It was good to spend time with her again. During the movie I started having labor pains in the theater. I guess the saying is true not to watch scary movies while you are pregnant. Once I was home, I spent the time trying to rest and breathe through the pain. My contractions were not close enough, and it seemed like the baby would never come. Since it seemed like it would be awhile before I needed to go to the hospital, my baby's father left to run some errands. As soon as he left, the contractions sped up. We did not have the convenience of cell phones. I had to call his family members to see if they could reach him. Just when I was going to call an ambulance, he showed up. I was in labor for over 24 hours. I was proud to have had a healthy baby boy naturally because I was determined not to endanger him with any medications. What I was not ready for was the pain I had to endure during labor and bringing him into this world. I tore and hemorrhaged which made me very weak. Due to the lack of strength, I could not hold my son for long. When I did hold him, I investigated his little face, and my heart burst with love. I remember thinking before I passed out, finally, I am no longer alone.

I was too weak to go home alone with a baby. My son's father had to get back to school. My parents were driving to St. Louis to get us. The hospital made it clear that I could not be left alone since I could not care for the baby. When my son's father brought us home, he put the baby in the bed with me and told me he could not wait for my parents to arrive. He left the door unlocked for them to get in on his way out. I was able to nurse my son without any problems since he was sleeping on my chest. I could also buzz my parents in the building since the phone was next to me. I could not do anything else. When my parents arrived, they were so angry he was not there, nor did he call their house to check on us when he made it back to school. That is when something broke inside of me for him.

CHAPTER 8

Life Saver

I know it may sound strange for me to say but, having my son was the best thing that could have happened. I was a 21 years old, single mom, college dropout, but I felt invincible. He breathed new life in me and honestly, I had a reason to dream and fight. He gave me purpose. All I wanted to do was give him the best life I could. I was not on public assistance and was proud of that fact. I had an office job at May Company in their New Accounts department. When I returned from maternity leave, I was working in their Support Department. I found a daycare not far from my job inside of a Catholic Church. I felt like the planets were aligning. God's blessings were falling over me.

I had my struggles. I was not rich but seeing his little smile and hearing his laugh made me happy. There was someone in my life I could love unconditionally, and I did not have to worry about any heartbreak behind it. Working at May Company, I received a lot of discounts and I gave my baby the best I could afford. I moved to a nicer apartment in a better neighborhood. Things seemed to be looking up.

School was my issue. I wanted to finish so I could provide a better life for him. We were not in a bad area, but I wanted a house and car. I was promoted on my job, but the stress level in that position caused problems. They promoted me to a collector. The stress of meeting their guidelines was unbearable. I could not convince people that paying their credit card was more important than paying their rent. I was having a hard time meeting the quota. I finally understood what it meant to hate your job. I searched for other jobs, but I had little luck. The money was a little better but not worth the stress. After my sister came to visit me, we planned for me to relocate to Atlanta and live with her. This would give me the opportunity to finish school and have a better job.

Living in Atlanta was a hard transition for me because I came from a city where public transportation took me anywhere, I needed to go. In suburban parts of Atlanta, you needed to have your own transportation. My sister lived in Lithonia and there were no buses in her area. She got me hired at the post office as a seasonal clerk and I worked there for a year on the 2nd shift. I worked long 10-hour days, 6 days per week with 1 off day. By the time I came home, I was exhausted. To say It was an adjustment, would be an understatement. I did not have a lot of time with my son or for myself and that was hard on both of us. He would cry every time I had to leave, and I felt sick for leaving him. Both my sister and my brother-in-law worked at the post office. They worked different shifts. Initially, I got a ride to work from them but eventually I met people that lived in the area and started getting rides to and from work with them.

As hard as those times were, things took a turn for the worst. We got a new supervisor at work and she had a not so pleasant history with my sister. Since I never gave her a reason to come for me, she would try and create one. I would be isolated in areas with tons of work to complete on my own. If I did not meet the deadline, I was written up. The rest of my team was sent in areas to complete work together. When her superior noticed what was happening, he called her into his office. He already knew my side of the story and wanted hers. I was there as well. She was happy to tell him because she thought I would be fired. As he listened, he told her he felt as if she had a personal problem with me. He informed her that he had been taking notice for weeks and could not understand her methods. He excused me from the office and furloughed me for one day, only to switch me to 3rd shift. This made it harder to spend time with my son. When he was waking up, I was going to sleep. Things with my sister got messy too. When I tried to go somewhere at night on my only off day that did not include my son, it did not sit well with my sister. I decided the best thing for me to do was to move back home. I took my son to his grandmother and father in Texas to help make the transition easier. Then I planned my move back to St. Louis. I got my old job back and an affordable place perfect for me and my baby boy. I thought this was a smart move. I would have more time for my son and work normal hours. Unfortunately, plans do not always work out how you want them too.

I saved money while I was in Atlanta to purchase a car, which was perfect since my old company moved from downtown St. Louis, to Earth City, a municipality that is approximately 20 minutes west of St. Louis. An area public transportation did not run. I went back to St. Louis, set up a townhome for us and enrolled back in school. Everything seemed perfect and as I was planning to bring my son back home when my townhome was broken into. This happened within the first few weeks of me being there.

I had just gone to bed and I noticed the kitchen light had come on. I did not hear anyone come in. So, I called out "who's there?" No one answered but I heard movement. I immediately called the police and directly after, I started calling anyone I thought could keep me company. I could not reach my closest friend who helped me find this place, so I left a message with her mom. Then I remembered my old co-worker from May Co went to work for St. Louis County Law Enforcement. Luckily for me, he was in the area at a party and made it there before the police arrived. When I went downstairs, my front and back doors were open. I noticed the speakers to my stereo were pulled out. I assumed they tried to disassemble them. My cell phone, spare car keys and a custom wooden box my father made was stolen. I was a complete mental and emotional mess.

RELEASED

While answering the officer's questions, the property security officer came in suited up and introduced himself. He said along with being property security he was also an officer for Pine Lawn Police Dept, a suburb near where I lived. As he passed me his card, my friend took it, and the officer asked, " who are you?" The tone was offensive, and I did not understand what was going on. We answered his questions, the locks were changed, and he left. My friend stayed because I was a mess. Neither one of us slept. We just listened to anything we could hear. My friend left when the sun came up, so I decided to call my co-worker and explain what happened. Although I owned a cell phone, they were not popular then. We had landline phones in our apartments. I had more than one phone in my townhome, but they shared the same line. I kept one in my bedroom and one in my kitchen. While we were talking, we heard someone else pick up the second phone line. I asked her if someone needed to use her phone and she said she has only one phone and she was on it. We both screamed. That meant someone was back in my townhome. I heard the door slam, felt the floor shake under my feet, and no one occupied the unit next to me. She called the police and so did I. After making another report, several of my friends drove up and packed my stuff. I was not staying there another day. In the next set of townhomes, there were guys yelling out of the windows facing us as we loaded up the cars, saying "Aww don't leave!" We only left the furniture.

    I stayed with friends for a while until the leasing office could find another unit in the front of the complex to put me in. Once settled in the new place, I did not feel safe enough to bring my son there. His dad was okay with him staying a little longer. I was sick without my son but refused to put him in danger.

Since I could not sleep there, I asked my childhood best friend from the 6th grade to move in with me. He did. I felt better knowing there was a guy in the house. He noticed things about the security officer I met the night of the break-in. He would always find a reason to stop by and when he did, he would question him about being there. Eventually, the officer caught me coming in from work and told me my roommate was selling drugs out of my townhome. I knew that was not true, but I wanted to see what was going on. He told me how my place is under surveillance and I could be put out for having him there. He had access to the tenant's files and showed me mine. He was trying to prove he knew my friend did not live there. When I went home to talk to my roommate, he said something is shady about the guy. He kept coming around asking him questions, wanting his name and his purpose of being there. My best friend left because he did not want to cause any problems, but he was concerned about me remaining there. I remember he told me to watch my back.

Once again, I was alone. I put extra security around my doors and went back to having sleepless nights. The first thing I noticed is my back light was out... a lot. The parking was behind the townhome, so I always left that light on because there were some days I worked late. I noticed it being out quite a bit. Secondly, my home phone was disconnected. When I called the phone company to find out why, they told me they received an anonymous call about the person who opened the account (my roommate) does not live there. In order to have a landline phone in your name, you had to be a resident of that property. Since I was still paying off my phone bill I had to close when I suddenly moved, and my cell phone was stolen, I was without a phone. I realized the only person who could have done this was the security guy. The final straw was when I came home after working a half-day on a Saturday. I ran in the house to change clothes and when I returned, I had a tow sticker on my car window. It said my car would be towed within 24 hours for having invalid license plates. My plates were new and legal. I was a student and because of that, legally, I did not have to change my plates to Missouri. I was so upset I went to a friend's house and told her what was going on. We decided I needed to see an attorney to get out of this lease.

    I found an attorney to take my case through legal aid. My consultation was free. I brought all the evidence I had. The "security officer's" card, the sticker from my car and I told her all that had taken place. I begged her for her help because I had nowhere else to turn. She said she will investigate this and get back to me. She called me the next day with an urgent message for me to come to her office. I went back to her office to see her. She informed me that the security officer has been suspended from the Pine Lawn Police Dept for stalking single women. He also had a couple of assault charges pending against him. She told me to leave that apartment immediately and not return. It is not safe for me to be there. She would sue the apartment complex for endangering me by having him as an employee. I told her all I wanted was to be out of my lease. I had no money to pay her because I was not working consistently due to the stress of this situation. I was falling behind on all my bills for missing work. I was having anxiety attacks. I was not sleeping. My stomach was hurting all the time and I was doing horribly on my job. I had not been there long enough to take time off so I could deal with the situation properly. I told her if she gets something from the lawsuit, it is hers. My friend met me at my apartment that day, and we packed all my belongings to move them into her basement. I moved in with her until my parents moved me to Cincinnati, OH.

In the meantime, I was at a low. I had lost everything. My new place for my son and I turned into a nightmare. I was given the option to resign from my job considering my circumstances. Without my job I could not afford my car, which I surrendered. The icing on the cake, I was moving back home with my parents. I felt like a complete failure to myself and my son. Waiting on my bus, I was in deep thought about how all of this happened in less than 6 months. Just when I thought things could not get any worse, a car pulled up in front of me. My abusive ex who I once worked with at the pizza place, rolled down his window all smiles. "Hey! What are you doing out here? You need a ride?" I was instantly ready to fight. "No!" I said. He got out of the car and I stepped back. He kept smiling. "How have you been?" My bus was coming.

"I'm fine." He offered a ride again and I declined. The bus pulled up and blew the horn since he was blocking the stop. I ran and hopped on the bus. My only thoughts were, I cannot wait to get out of this city.

CHAPTER 9

Contact

My dad was eventually laid off from his job in Virginia not long after my parents moved there. They relocated to Cincinnati for another job opportunity. Initially, I was in a funk. I did not talk much and all I could see was what I lost. Very quickly though, I realized it turned out to be a blessing to be able to come home. The house was beautiful. Although the house itself was not familiar, the familiarity came from the smell of the house, the furnishings and my parents made it home. There was a sense of peace there. I slept without worrying someone would be standing over me or breaking in. I could come home without feeling like I had to run from my car to the house. After a few days, I knew this was the right move to get back on my feet. But, even with all those comforts, I knew I could not stay.

I had not been home to live since I left when I was 18 years old. I was now 24 years old. There was still something about being back home that made me feel like I was a failure. I was wondering if I should have stayed in Atlanta. I had a car and I am sure my sister would have helped me find a one-bedroom apartment. I guess I thought there was something left for me in St. Louis. Now I know, there was not. Other than a few friends, St. Louis was dead to me. Now that I was in Cincinnati, OH, I still had to establish myself to bring my son home. I had been without him too long and I felt sick without him. I came up with a plan to get on my feet and reboot my life.

I lost my car when I was in St. Louis because I missed too much work dealing with the stress of a stalker while I was there. Luckily, Cincinnati was more like St. Louis in the way of transportation. I found bus routes that got me to my job without a problem. My Dad would take me or pick me up if the weather were too bad. Once I knew I had the first job on lock, I found a 2nd one. I left no room to get comfortable. I consolidated all my bills that fell behind, and I was also responsible for the utilities on the floor I lived on.

My parents had a huge 3 story home with a basement. The 3rd floor was not used. It was set up like an apartment. There were 2 bedrooms, a living room and a full bathroom. There was a separate utility bill for that floor that was my responsibility. My mother did not play about her bills. If I was short on money for any reason, it was not her bill that was shorted. I also had to make sure my mother knew what my plan was. I could not just come home and leave whenever. She had to know how long this transition would be. With all my debt, I gave reestablishing myself 2 years. I did not see my parents often since I worked 2 jobs. As I did, I bought new Living Room furniture, dishes, pots and pans and stored everything in the garage with the rest of my stuff. I knew once I moved, I would not be able to afford to buy these items and pay rent.

One thing for sure, I was determined. Rain, sleet or snow I was grinding. My dad tried to teach me how to drive his car, which had a manual transmission. That did not go so well. I kept getting stuck and felt like I was going to burn out his clutch. I eventually bought another car, which allowed me to find a better paying 2nd job. I met new friends on my jobs and hung out from time to time, but it did not fill the void of me missing my son. Nothing did. I called him all the time and his dad brought him to Cincinnati to visit. I missed his little body and his little smell. He was my everything and the drive I needed to push harder. Between both jobs I worked 7 days a week. I was in Cincinnati for 2 years when I received a call from a friend in Atlanta.

I kept in touch with a girlfriend I used to work with at the post office. She was in the circle of people I hung out with. One guy from that circle was looking to contact me and she wanted to know was it okay to give him my number. I did not know for what reason, but I okayed it. He was one of the guys that was married, so imagine my surprise when he told me he was divorced and wanted to pursue a relationship with me. I reminded him I no longer resided in Atlanta and I was not planning to come back. He said he would try and change my mind. He called me daily and worked around my schedule making sure he reached me. Our friendship grew. He eventually came to Cincinnati to see me and meet my parents. He was a little intimidated to learn my father was a Bishop. I also noticed it made him more determined for us to be together. He asked me to move in with him. I liked him but I was not sure that was the route I wanted to take. He was persistent. I knew his offer was genuine, but I also knew he was dealing with some drama from his ex-wife. That was something I wanted no part of. I talked to my dad about it and his advice was " a man will clean up his mess and make a place for you. He won't drag you through it with him." He told me if it were meant for us to be together, we would be.

CHAPTER 10

The Arrangement

I have heard all my life a hard head makes a soft behind. Deep inside I was lonely. It had been years since I connected with someone. Being home watching my parents interact, made me want to be loved. The closest I came to that feeling was high school. It was almost 10 years later. Maybe this is the real thing. He seemed to be putting forth the effort and he was excited about meeting my son. Ignoring my dad's advice, I moved to Atlanta, instead of waiting. I knew my 2-year timeline was reached and I was about to get my own place anyway. When I first got to Atlanta, he was in a roommate situation with his co-worker. It was slightly awkward considering I had never lived with anyone but my family. The lease was close to ending and we were going to get our own place. Of course, this is when I found out he had a lot of debt and he had not been paying his bill as he should. I was able to lock in a place for us, which worked out for our benefit because I came home from work one day to see we were being evicted. His roommate had already moved out and since my name was not on anything, I could not inquire about what was happening. He claimed he did not know about it and never saw a notice. I did not argue since I had just moved there and had not seen an eviction notice either.

We stayed at his mom's house until the new place was ready. She was polite, but she was a fan of his ex-wife. His brother lived there as well, which means his girlfriend and their son were there often. We stayed in the spare bedroom downstairs. I tried to go straight there when I came in from work just to keep the awkward looks and conversations from happening. Although it was a short stay at his mom's until we moved into the new place, there seemed to be a few small incidents he seemed to smoothly sweep under the rug. For example, an old coworker from the post office, who had an interest in him was in the group of friends we met up with one night. She loudly bad talked me to him asking him why he was with me and he just laughed it off. Later telling me he does not need to answer to anyone about what he is doing. She was nobody, so he ignored her. I felt it was a lame excuse. I felt he should have checked her about me, informing her of who I was to him. That is something I should not have to tell him. I did not want to seem paranoid, but I started to see a different side of him.

What should have also been an eye-opener for me was the incident with his brother being physically abusive towards his girlfriend, while their toddler screamed. When I heard the arguing, I did not think much of it since his brother's girlfriend was full of drama. When she came over yelling, I just assumed it was a regular day. I had not been there that long and already learned that behavior was the norm. However, when his mom called him for some help, I knew something else was happening. When we went upstairs, his mother was trying to pull his brother off his girlfriend. The problem was he had her braids wrapped around his hand, pulling them from her head. Their son was jumping up and down crying at the top of his lungs and I quickly grabbed him and left the room. We went downstairs and I tried to calm him down. As soon as I did, the girlfriend came running downstairs to grab a butcher knife from the drawer. I was holding the toddler as the girl tried to go slash his motorcycle tires. His mother blocked the door to the garage and told her nothing is going to be being cut in this house. She was holding the knife on the mother, telling her to move. Screaming she bought the bike and he will not be riding it to his other chick's house. His brother came downstairs after her and she turns the knife on him. More ugly words were exchanged. His mother told her to leave, saying they need some cooling off time. She threatened him, grabbed her son and left, tearing out of the driveway. His brother went back upstairs, and his mom said, she should not do the things she does to make him angry and she would not have to be hit. I slowly turned and looked at her as if I were seeing her for the first time. I asked her was she serious? "There is NO reason a man should be beating on a woman." She just looked at me as if I was a fool. I later asked him what his mother meant by that, and he told me his father used to beat on her in front of them. His parents may not have lived together anymore but they were still married. He had his life and she still committed to him as his wife. She sent meals to his home by one of the boys and made sure he had his medicine when he was ill. I immediately thought back to my crazy ex and wondered how I got here again? But was I? He showed no signs of anger and rage such as that. Yes, it can be hereditary, but it does not mean every child will be that way. He was nothing like his brother. He was more like a gentle giant.

I thought moving into the new place would be a new start for us. We were away from the drama and the influence of his family. We could finally get settled and my baby could come home. It was fine for a few months, but then things changed. He worked part-time with a security team on the weekends at various clubs and events. I really did not know many people in Atlanta. Sometimes he would bring me with him to the club just so I could get out of the house. I have never been a club person, so I did not dress for the club. Jeans and t-shirts or sweatshirts were all that I wore. I would either sit in the car or on the side steps not far from the entrance. I would people watch, looking at the different women with slinky barely-there dresses and heels trying to get in free before the cut off time. There was a popular radio personality who would step outside before things really got started. He would hang out on the side stairs as well and eventually we became cool. Having someone to talk to help the time go by. Sometimes he would bring us some wings and fries to eat while we chatted it up. I remember one night my boyfriend walked up and said I need to go sit in the car. He cut the DJ a nasty look. I assured him I was fine, but he looked angry and insisted I sit in the car. After he walked away, the DJ asked me why I was dating him. He said something about my boyfriend did not feel right to him and I needed to be careful. I appreciated the DJ's concern, but I never saw a reason to be worried. He may be a little jealous about how close we seemed to have gotten, but he was harmless. The DJ offered his truck for me to go home and he would get it from me later. I explained it would not be appropriate and besides, I did not know how to get home. I was not that familiar with Atlanta. I told him the area we lived in, but that is all I knew. He shook his head and said I was not safe with dude and to be careful. The next weekend I was ready to go, and he told me I was not going anymore. I could not understand why, and all my boyfriend said was to figure it out. I never saw that DJ again in person. However, a year or so later I bought a cd of a rapper I had been hearing a lot about on the radio. I loved his music. Come to find out, it was the DJ from the club. His name as a radio personality was different. He had become a famous rapper and later a famous actor.

A couple of months later, the holidays rolled around, and I received a diamond ring from him. I was thinking he is finally making good on the type of relationship he claimed he wanted with me, but before I could get too excited, he said,

"It's not that type of ring." When I later spoke to my parents, my dad asked to speak to him. When he did, my dad asked him, " What are your plans with my daughter? You came to my home, you moved her out, but I do not see you making future with her." They talked for a while. Once my boyfriend was off the phone, he told me about the conversation and asked me what I wanted to do. I told him the plan was for us to get married and he said fine, let us do it. It was more like a business arrangement than a proposal. There was nothing romantic about it. It sounded more like doing the right thing after speaking with my dad. We planned a wedding. We took care of the invitations, playlist, and attire. I went to find an engagement ring, put it on layaway. Later we picked out bands. My parents took care of the wedding since it was being held in Ohio.

In May 1999, we were married in Cincinnati, OH. It was a beautiful church to have the wedding in, with a few friends and family. Nothing fancy. My son's father refused to come to the wedding, which meant my son was not there. That was heartbreaking to me. Two of my friends were by my side, and a friend and my brother-in-law were by his side. I was kind of happy his brother was not there. He would not have meshed well with my people. My then best friend refused to come, saying there were two things she did not do, weddings and funerals. The day of the wedding she called to apologize. She claimed jealousy. It was hurtful but I forgave her. My brother walked me down the aisle since my father officiated the wedding. I cried from the moment I got dressed until I was standing side by side with my future husband, facing my father. I had no reason for my behavior, nor did I know why I was crying but it put everyone on edge. Everyone kept pulling me to the side asking me if I wanted to marry him. His mother was getting angry, walking around saying, "if she doesn't want to marry my baby…" I felt no doubts. Honestly, it felt weird. I did not feel overjoyed with happiness. Maybe I was in shock. I was simply happy we made it through the ceremony. Once the ceremony was over. I stopped being emotional completely. It was done. Then everything that could go wrong, did. The food never arrived, so they ran out to get chicken from Popeyes. The photographer/ videographer was drunk, which means all pictures were lost or destroyed and the video did not have sound. It also had a green filter over the entire footage. If it were not for all the little disposable cameras on the tables, I would not have had any pictures. Finally, the wedding night did not happen. I mean there was a night for the wedding, but nothing happened with us. We slept apart, got on the road the next day after saying thank you and goodbye to my parents, friends and family and started on a path of matrimony I did not expect.

— CHAPTER 11 —

The Awakening

Returning to Atlanta began an exciting time. Everything was new for me. I was a wife now. That meant a lot of responsibility as a woman. I knew you could not treat your husband like a boyfriend. I had to give him the respect, trust and love he deserved. I also had to treat him like the head of our family that he was. Instead of me being closed off and handling our business without him, I had to discuss things with him first and come to a mutual agreement. I have seen my parents do this plenty of times. I knew I could do this. I quickly learned, he did not care about household business and bills. He told me to let him know how much money I needed and that was it. He was more interested in searching for a new home and getting new vehicles. He also got along well with my son since he knew how to play video games. and how to work on cars, which he liked to watch his dad and uncle do. Mostly, things seemed to be going smoothly on the surface, but then some cracks showed.

His old co-worker, the disrespectful one, reared her ugly head again. She called our house looking for my husband and when I answered, she immediately got smart. I told her do not call our house again because I am no longer a girlfriend, I am his wife. She did not know we had married. She called me a liar and continued to fuss. I hung up. This started a series of problems. She obviously reached him somehow because when he came home, he had an attitude. I asked him how she got our phone number and he claimed she must have gotten it from a mutual friend. I told him about the disrespectful call, and he argued back saying she was just a friend. I knew he was lying, and he knew I did not believe him. This was the first time he got in my face trying to intimidate me. When that did not work. He spoke to me like I was less than. That was all too familiar.

Shortly following that incident, I came home early from work sick with the flu. His ex-wife was waiting in the parking lot of our apartment complex with her fiancé. She recognized me as soon as I pulled up. She called me by my new last name and approached me, introducing herself. She obviously had done her homework. She was looking for him, claiming he had stolen money from her. I did not know what she was talking about and when she realized I was telling the truth, she explained. The house they had together was left to her. She was getting remarried and had gotten the house refinanced.

Since the house and insurance were in both of their names, the escrow check was automatically sent to him since he was the primary on the accounts. He had been gone for a couple of years and they had not had the house long before he left. She was paying for the house and rightfully the money should have been hers. I told her I would let him know she was trying to reach him. In confronting him about having thousands of dollars tucked away, he said he spent it all by going out to eat. I knew he was lying. I made breakfast, lunch, and dinner for him daily. The fact that he would keep something like this from me made me wonder what else he would hide. He claimed he would talk to her and work everything out. I never found out how that ended.

After something bad or shady would happen, he would become loving and helpful. He would buy me red roses, suddenly becoming thoughtful. I knew they were guilt flowers. Our marriage was new. I wanted to believe he was trying. However, there was always another incident. One day I was home and heard a chirping noise in the house. I thought maybe an insect had gotten in. I followed the noise to our bedroom, and it was coming from a briefcase he had left on the floor. I opened it to find a cell phone going dead. I knew it was not his cell phone. I turned it off and put it back in his briefcase. I asked him about it later and he claimed it was his brother's phone. The next week before I left for work, I was leaving a note in his truck as my car warmed up. His truck sat high and I hopped inside the cab with my legs hanging out the opened door trying not to freeze. I tried to stick the note to his steering wheel, and it fell to the floor. Since I leave before the sun is fully up, I had to feel around on the floor for the sticky since it was dark, and his dome light was not much help. His truck was always junky with magazines and newspapers on the floor. When I thought I felt it, I pulled up a paper that was a page for a phone bill in his name. Bringing it closer to the light, he had called the same number and had long conversations (over an hour) regularly with the same person. I immediately went back into the house, asking him about this. He claimed he got the phone for his brother and the bill came to him. The times coordinated with his work schedule. Although I was not convinced, I had no other proof. His brother always covered for him.

I tried to turn things around and lead by example. This was a marriage and when you are married, you are supposed to fight for it, right? Well his birthday was coming up and I had been paying attention to things he showed interest in. I left work and went to his job to decorate his truck. I filled it with balloons and put a happy birthday sign in the window. I even had flowers delivered to him. That was different. I had gifts for him at home and I cooked one of his favorite dinners. One thing he loved was attention. He loved all his gifts. I worked hard to surprise him, and it worked. I did everything I knew to make things better. Sometimes it worked and sometimes it did not. I noticed I was the only one putting forth the effort. He went along for the ride. My birthday came around that year on a weekend. I did not receive so much as a card. He was lying in bed that afternoon about to take a nap, when I asked him about it, and he said he had no money. He claimed I took it all for bills. I was shocked. He did not acknowledge me at all. I told him my birthday is the same every year. I cannot believe he did nothing. Not even a happy birthday. I was crushed. For someone who worked two jobs, and still had time to hang out with his brother, he did not have time to think of me for my birthday. I was done.

Because problems kept popping up, we grew distant. We were not talking, the arguing and his nasty comments continued, the attempts to bully and intimidate me had gotten worse. I ignored him when I got angry because I hated arguing. They always teetered on violence. He would walk on my heels fussing like he was looking for an excuse to do something. I ended that quickly when he used his body to bump me from behind while I was ignoring him during an argument. To get to the laundry room, I had a walk through the kitchen. I stumbled with the clothes basket in hand, dropped it to the floor and in the same move picked up the cast-iron skillet and told him that if he didn't back up off of me, his mama may have never seen where he lived but she will know where he died. I was tired of his intimidation moves and nasty words. The only fight I had in me was for my life.

Things became quiet after that. There were not any incidents for a while. The arguing calmed down, but there was still tension and distance. Holidays came and went like another day. He did not acknowledge it. I did not either. I took vacation time and drove back home to St. Louis. I spent time with my closest friends and even saw the guy I dated through high school. It was not easy hearing about his marriage and children, regardless, it was nice seeing him again. It was nice having someone to spend time with and talk to that did not end in an argument.

I felt isolated in my own home. I did not have many friends because the couple of friends I had when I met him, he decided were not the right type of people I should be hanging out with now that I am married. This was the same friend he contacted to get in touch with me when I lived in Cincinnati. We talked about what to do next because he knew I was at the end of my rope. He said he would do better, and for a while, he did. We bought a house. During the unpacking phase of the move, I ran across his divorce decree. The date on the decree was one year after we had been married. My heart stopped. I called my attorney immediately and asked him if this meant we were not married. He said no, our marriage became legal when his other marriage ended. It was easy for him to do since it was in another state. I never mentioned it because I did not want to put him on guard. I kept looking through our file cabinet and I noticed he had filed our bank statements away, which is unusual. I looked them over and noticed double check numbers. I called the bank and checks had been written for cash withdrawals. I told them it was fraud because I have all our starter checks. I was the only one who wrote checks. I went in and showed them my check recorder. We closed the account. I later found a second set of starter checks with the used carbon copies matching every withdrawal from our account filed in another section of our file cabinet. It seemed like everything I thought I knew about him was a lie.

Our schedules did not allow us to spend time together nor did we see each other during the week. When I was up going, he was sleeping and vice versa. One night I remember hearing laughter in the house, and I thought it was because he was watching television. Our bedroom phone had a light on it if there was a line in use. He was on the phone talking to someone at 2:00 in the morning. When I picked up the line, I heard a woman's voice, and then he hung up, and when she heard the click, she hung up too. I confronted him and the argument started. During the argument, he grabbed me by my arms, forcefully shaking me as he yelled and cursed. I was pushing away, trying to get loose. I was in fight or flight mode. When one arm got free, he grabbed my neck, and I swung blindly. He was taller and bigger than me, but I was a fighter. I twisted, kicked, and swung until I connected with something that allowed him to let me go free. Once I was loose, I was reaching for the 1st thing to knock him out. He asked me if I really wanted to do this, and I said if you put your hands on me again, yes. He left the house and I noticed through the reflection of the mirror, my son sitting on the stairs, watching. I grabbed him while running upstairs and locked the bedroom door.

Even though he was cheating, he treated me like the villain. There were more violent incidents like this to follow. One afternoon, I left the house and drove to our church to talk to someone. I believed the church would help me. It was the place to take refuge. The staff member I ran into said the pastor who completed our premarital counseling was not available and asked how she could help. I cried and explained what I was going through, pulling up my sleeve to reveal the bruises. She stepped back saying, "What are you still doing there?" The look on her face was accusatory. I was taken aback. I told her I did not know where to go, and I was looking for help. Looking for someone to talk to. She said that I needed to call someone and get out of there. She did not offer comfort or any spiritual guidance. Wasn't that what the church was for? The people? I felt like leaning on the church was a waste of time. I felt as if everyone looked at me as if I were the fool for being there. Maybe I was. I left wondering what my next steps should be. I did not have to wait long. I received proof of his infidelity, and that is when things turned a corner.

There was a bad storm that made me think the phone lines in the house were crossed. I was on the phone with a friend when the phone kept ringing upstairs. When I answered it, a woman asked for my husband. I took a message and went about my business. I did not think anything of it because people called all the time for him to work on their cars. Once I was settled back into my conversation, the phone rang again. I did the same thing. By the 3rd time, I was wondering about the phone lines. We had an office with a separate phone line for the internet. The thing was it never rang because it was connected to the computer. My friend told me if something were wrong with the phone lines, we could not talk. So, I checked, and he had switched the cords. He plugged a phone up to the computer line to make calls. These women were women he was seeing. That night, our mutual friend who we both worked with at the post office told me she had heard about him messing with a woman on his job. She was still in touch with some of the old crew we all hung out with. She thought nothing of it since I did not complain to her. Now this was happening, she knew it to be true. Apparently, there was a woman he had been seeing for a while and she was under the impression we were getting a divorce. She knew things about me she should not know.

That night I did not sleep. I thought about my life and what I wanted. I went into a different mindset of being single. When he came home. I confronted him. He denied it until he could not. He slipped and said she needed him. She needed someone to talk to. I had been sitting in a house day after day alone, and she needed him. My husband who isolated me. He made me feel unattractive and would not touch me. The husband who had every excuse to not be home but expected me to stay there. The husband who was so paranoid of me running around town, he checked my mileage daily and made me feel like a prisoner in our own home. I just looked at him like he was nothing. He was not worth any more breath. I went to the bedroom and rested until it was time for work. He left. I was fine with that. When I was leaving for work, there was a card on the counter, apologizing. I left it. I got in my car, and there was a rose and card on my seat, apologizing. I threw it out. I got to work, and later that day, three dozen long-stemmed red roses were delivered. Everyone thought he was so sweet. For every woman that said that I gave her a bouquet of flowers. I did not want them or the man they came from.

He continued to apologize. He was home all the time now. I agreed to counseling, but after the first meeting, he left early, angry. He said he was never going back. There were many more arguments in days to follow, waking up with bruises here and there. Several times the police were called out to our home. We could not put one another out without a restraining order due to both of us owning the house. One night when the police were there, he volunteered to leave the house but told the police he was afraid to get his things because I was upstairs with his gun. He kept a 9MM in the case, in our closet. I never pulled his gun out and to try and make me seem like I would to the officers, pissed me off. The police ended up searching the house and right before they went into my son's room, who was sleeping, I stopped them and said, do not shine that light in my son's room. I pointed to our room and the closet. They retrieved the gun and told him he was welcome to pack his things.

As time passed, he stopped by the house to retrieve things or slept there when I was gone, but he also tampered with the alarm system changing the code, put a recording device on our home phone line and slowly stopped paying for things in the house. He was also using our computer phone line for his personal calls again. After confronting him about illegally recording my calls and messing with the alarm, we had one of the worst fights. Things were broken, threats were made, and my son was in the bath screaming out, "you better not hurt my mommy!" I knew at that moment our marriage was over. It was beyond repair.

CHAPTER 12

Getting Free

As I was planning to free myself from this situation, I called home numerous times to talk to my parents about some of the problems I was having in my marriage. I was trying to find a way to tell them I wanted a divorce. I wanted their blessings. I did not have any support from my mom. She told me I was being spoiled and just used to getting my way. She did not believe he was doing those things. Most people did not. He was charming. Full of smiles and friendly conversation. He helped people often and many times did not accept payment from them for any work he did. But in our 4 walls he was not so nice. There were no smiles or friendly conversations. It was cold in our home and my son had started calling him The Mean Man.

One of my closest friends back home in St. Louis stopped

speaking to me if I was still with him. I knew she was tired of hearing about me going through this, but she did not understand marriage was different from having a boyfriend. You do not just break up because things get a little rough. So, when my parents came to town, I took advantage of the opportunity to talk to my closest confidant, my daddy. I told him what was happening and what I was planning. My daddy was the best listener and gave the best advice. He told me if I did not feel safe and I have tried everything, I need to pray and walk out on faith. It did not make sense to remain in a loveless abusive marriage. Nothing good will come out of it. I loved my talks with my dad, and I felt better about my next moves. I finally felt hope and direction. However, that was short-lived.

When I got off work that night, my sister called me to tell me our daddy was in the hospital. My father passed away from an aneurysm 24 hours later. I had lost my best friend. The first man to ever love me unconditionally, my life was falling apart. We held his funeral in Chattanooga, Tennessee. Since he was retired from the Navy, it was a Military Funeral Honors. During the services, it was one of the hardest days of my life. I was distraught and blinded by tears. I knew my brother was holding me up, but I did not realize he had passed me off to someone to be there for my mother. I did not realize it was my soon to be ex who was holding me until it was time to exit the funeral home. I jumped away as if the devil were holding me himself. I may have been mourning, but my heart and mind were the same with him. His mother was with him and became angry because I refused to see or talk to him. I do not know how he found out about my father's funeral. He was trying to use my time of weakness to slither back in, which did not work.

Going forward, he stayed at his mother's. I held on to my daddy's words. While I was working a 2nd shift job, I used the mornings to separate everything in the house. I divided everything into tubs, created an itemized list with columns of what was his and mine. He signed it and I turned it in to my attorney when I filed for divorce. Later that day, after I met with my attorney, I met with the real estate agent who sold us the house to put it back on the market after one year of owning it. When my soon to be ex saw the sign in the yard, he was enraged. He offered to buy it from me, but he had no money and his credit would not allow for a refinance.

Things became worse when he was served with the divorce papers. He called me repeatedly, screaming and cursing. I would hang up every time. He got an attorney and tried to stall the divorce by contesting the dividing of the property, which he signed off on. It did not work.

While this was happening, a buyer made an offer on the house. I scraped together every dime I had to get the house ready. At the closing, I needed to pay a difference after the sale that I did not have. I was terrified this would happen. My soon to be ex burst out laughing hysterically at the table. My realtor asked the buyer's realtor to step in the hallway. The buyer and I sat at the table in an awkward moment as the laughter died down. We waited on the agents to finish talking. Nothing was said between us. When the agents returned, they had agreed upon a way to cover the cost I had to pay. My agent forgoes his commission and the other agent forgoes a portion of hers. When this was said, tears ran down my cheeks, I was so happy. The buyer signed the paperwork first, I signed next and my soon-to-be ex signed last. When he finished, he tossed the pen, stood and slammed the chair against the table. The woman agent and I jumped, startled by the noise. Everyone looked over at him as he stalked out of the room and slammed the door. Then the women agent took my hand and said you are free now. I cried because the kind gesture, coupled with what they sacrificed, was only something God could deliver.

Two months later was our court date to finalize the divorce. All his efforts to stall an uncontested divorce did not work. He was given 30 days to sign the divorce papers, and he waited until the 30th day. The day we were due in court, he did not show. I was so happy. When the judge granted the divorce and to change my name back to my maiden name, I asked him could I hug him. My attorney and I immediately went downstairs and obtained my divorce decree. Once I was in my car, I could not stop praising God for being free. I checked my phone, and he had called leaving a screaming voicemail of why I did not remind him that today we had to be in court. All I could do was laugh. I was completely free.

I immediately updated everything with my maiden name. I was not ready to live on my own, so my brother and I became roommates. After the move, my son asked me, "was the mean man gone?" I told him yes. The mean man is gone out of our lives forever. It felt so good to be out of that house and away from all the problems.

CHAPTER 13

Staying Strong

I was starting a new chapter in my life. I had to find the strength to carry on without my daddy. I was finally in a safe place. I could sleep without being startled awake. I could come home without having to look for any surprises. The bruises had all healed on the outside but the scars on the inside were a permanent fixture.

I roomed with my brother for 2 years. He found us a roommate style apartment. I found a new job and things seemed to be going well. I had one incident with my ex threatening me. He called my sister telling her lies of me calling his girlfriend and telling her awful things about him. My sister knew I had not been in touch with him or anyone he knew. Listening to him go on about me, threatening me and saying he will fix this, told my sister he was crazy. My mother called me and suggested I get a restraining order against him. She told me to keep any voicemails he leaves me for evidence. I never did. I applied for a gun license instead. I was no longer his victim. Instead of him confronting me, he had other plans for me. He did not want to talk. He wanted me dead. He had found out where I worked, and on my way home he tried to run me off the road. The only way I could get away was to stay ahead of him because when he was on the side of me, he was guiding me off the road. There was no shoulder, only a drop off. I was weaving in and out of traffic trying to get away. He was driving a MAC tow truck. All I saw was the grill in my rearview mirror. He made every move I made. I could not shake him. I knew a backroad turn was coming up and I threw my emergency break up and slid into the turn. I pulled behind a Bank of America shaking uncontrollably. That was the last time I had any dealings with him.

I did not let that incident stop me from moving forward. I was still in school doing all I could to better myself. I was getting back to me. I dropped all the stress weight I gained; my hair stopped thinning out. And I realized I had way too much time on my hands. I was obtaining a psychology degree to become a counselor. The school required a few hours of hands-on experience, so I volunteered at a Rape Crisis Center in Grady Hospital. They were 12-hour shifts on the weekends. My first thought was how easy this would be. I had not heard anything about mass rapes. So, I was thinking maybe 1 or 2 per weekend. I quickly realized there could be 4-6 per night. In downtown Atlanta, there are 4 universities and plenty of clubs and plenty of opportunity for abuse. This was the city hospital, which means the worst cases came here. Many people did not have insurance. I volunteered here thinking I could give back since I am a survivor of the abuse I was seeing, and I did. It was about service, not my testimony. Our patients came in through the emergency room. Some walked in and a few were on stretchers.... nearly beaten to death. I stood alongside police officers obtaining the survivor's statements. Afterwards, I would support them during their rape kit exam, show them to a private place to shower, and offer fresh clothes. Some clothing would be used for evidence, some tossed and others to be taken home. Last, we assisted with transportation home and plenty of counseling information. I enjoyed working there, however, I wanted to help in more of a counseling capacity.

After a few months, I applied for an internship at Planned Parenthood. I was accepted to shadow the clinic manager and learn health education. I loved it! I was able to counsel patients about their bodies and options. It was rewarding and it changed my life. I realized psychology was not the way I wanted to go. Being on the preventative side as a health educator was all I wanted. I was approved to switch my shift at work on the days I had to intern. I stayed for a year, six months as an intern and 6 months as a paid employee. When management changed, so did my responsibilities and knew it was time to move on. I wanted to stick with counseling in some capacity, and I applied for a volunteer/internship at a group home.

I was hired on the weekends to work with troubled teens girls ages 7 – 17. I worked there for 2 years. I monitored, counseled and chaperoned the girls on outings. This was extremely rewarding work as well because I got to see the caterpillar become a beautiful butterfly. Many of these young ladies came from dysfunctional homes. Parents were on drugs or alcoholics, children were molested, abandoned and some were runaways. It was rewarding to work with them and help them through their pain. Many of these young ladies never had someone to care about them. They were used and mistreated. When they learned that I was coming from a genuine place, some allowed me to help them. Seeing them come from a place of depression to not needing their medications and succeeding in the program, told me the work the counselors were doing was worth it. Once some of the girls had moved on, I received a few thank you letters for being there for them. They would include pictures of how well they were doing. It was very emotional to hear about them thriving in the world and knowing I was a part of their success.

During the time of my volunteering and interning, I dated here and there. I dated a guy for about five months while interning at Planned Parenthood, that I met on my job. I came in earlier on those days and our third shift crew was still there. He introduced himself on the first day I switched my shift. He was easy to talk to and fun to be around. That was a nice change from the hell I had been through. I just took it day by day because I was focused on the life, I was building for myself and my son. It was a no-pressure kind of dating, which was peaceful. We grew close. When we went out, it was intense. It was like we knew each other for years. We talked for hours, shutting down restaurants, cruising the city just to get to know each other. Our first date was 24 hours without anything physical. It was nice. He eventually met my sister and brother and I met his family. He has a large family, and many were in town when we hung out for the first time. I was not ready to meet everyone but hanging out at the bowling alley was fun. We had breakfast at the Waffle House afterwards since it was the only thing open. Everyone was nice and friendly. Our relationship was a series of simple dates. He cooked for me. I cooked for him. A lot of family time and long nights of talking. I even met his daughter and helped her with her homework. We kept it low key at work. The blessing was the different shifts. He was thoughtful with little gifts if he had been out of town or to celebrate me being offered a permanent position at the clinic. I liked him being into me, but I was waiting for the other shoe to drop. This guy was the stereotypical type of guy that most females wanted. He had the hot boy look with the legit job and a sweetheart. I knew there was more to the story. Time always showed me. He shocked me when he took me to meet his mom. I did not know that was his plan, and I was dressed in sweats to run errands. I quickly learned that catching a person off guard must have been his thing. I was on pins and needles. She was very regal and strong. She sat posed in a high back chair, and when she spoke to me, it was like passing the exam of your life. She hit me with so many questions, you would have thought he was royalty. She asked me about myself, my future, and how I felt about her son. We had not known each other long. We connected immediately, and it felt like we had a deep history. I must have passed her test because he said she gave her approval of me. I talked to his mom a lot afterwards, but what I loved about her was her spirit. She prayed a lot and invited me to pray with her. I felt a peace that was much needed in my life. Things went smoothly with us until they did not. We went from smooth sailing to an abrupt stop. There were things going on with him and friends he confided in that I was not privy to. He was private in that way. I respected that and thought he would talk when he was ready. But he never did. Instead he decided for us to stop seeing each other. No explanation. No discussion. The only thing he said was "I love you. I am in love with you. But I can't be with you anymore." Done. It was hard to take to say the least because I was blindsided. We did not have arguments. Of course, we disagreed but we agreed to disagree and moved on. We were not in one another's space too much. We were not planning our lives together. His mother said his feelings were intense and he got cold feet because of the direction it was going. When he learned his mother was still in touch with me, he made sure that relationship ended as well. All ties were cut with him and his family. I was thankful for having a busy schedule, which kept me from having time to dwell on this.

It seemed like once I started counseling, friends and friends of friends would come to me for help and counseling. His mother called me one last time and asked me to counsel her other son's ex-girlfriend. She was in the hospital, depressed and on suicide watch. She was pregnant with twins. I did not want to get involved considering that would mean I still had some connection to his family. After talking to his mom more, I realized this is not about him. I worked with her. I started with phone calls and then I would drive almost an hour after leaving the clinic to sit with her on Saturdays. We became friends and she made me the godmother of her twin boys. When he found out, he was not happy about it. I tried to be there for her as much as I could. The babies were premature, and they had to remain at the hospital. I met her family. They were appreciative of my help with her. I began to purchase things for the babies. I was excited to help. I had been there for her through the summer and into fall when I met her brother. A lesson I learned while having a heart of helping people was to know where to draw the line.

I was not in the head space for another relationship, so I threw myself into helping others. When I was getting all the attention from her brother, I was vulnerable and still emotionally raw. I went too far and ended up with a beautiful baby girl. Although, being with my daughter's father was not right, having my daughter gave me a new look at life. Raising my son was different because we co-parented. His dad and I remained friends. We raised him to be a strong, respectful, responsible young man. His father had always been in his life. My son and I kind of grew up together. As I learned things, I educated him on many dos and don'ts dealing with these young ladies, friends, and life in general. He had a lot of guidance around him. His dad and I did very well together. He was an awesome kid. Successful in his sports, easy to make friends, maintained good grades. No matter what obstacles came his way, he had a village to help him overcome them.

The story with my daughter's father was the opposite. We did not get along at all. He was not the kind of guy I would typically be involved with. I knew he was a rebound. My ex who ended it abruptly knew the family and asked me why I would get involved with them. I was not thinking. I was in a vulnerable place. I wanted my daughter more than anything, but I wanted to raise her without the drama her dad and his family brought. I knew that was selfish of me. She had a right to know them. When I came to that conclusion, he ended up going to jail for a couple of years. I took her to see him twice per month. I tried to support him by assisting his parents with attorney fees and keeping him active in the temp service database just so he could land a job when he got out. I did not mind him being involved in her life, but he was inconsistent, which caused a lot of problems. When he came home and found a job, he offered to go in half on her daycare and after a few months he said she was not his and I should go find her real daddy. He asked for a paternity test. In Georgia, if you fail the test, you pay. He called me back to back. Once the test results came back, he must have known what that meant. This was something I never had to deal with. When I called the county office about a letter that was sent to me pertaining to processing child support, I told them I had no intention of doing so. They told me it was my daughter's right. He ended up on child support and he lost his mind about having to pay. We tried to work out visitation, but that went left as well. He would lie about where our daughter was or just disappear and not answer the phone. It turned ugly fast. The final straw was when I called to check on her since she was only 2 years old. She had been crying, and I could tell something was wrong. When I asked him, he was nonchalant as if it was no big deal. I knew differently. She did not cry for no reason. She was a happy baby. It turned ugly with him hanging up and not answering the phone. When we finally spoke again, he threatened to drop her off on my sister's doorstep and told me if I wanted her, I could pick her up there. My sister was out of town, and I had reached a new level of anger. Threatening him was too good for him. I was so angry he might not have lived to see the next day. At which point, his mother and brother brought her home. She was dirty, in a full pullup, which means he did not try to continue her potty training. She had on the same clothes from the day before. I overpacked for her with a new pack of pullups and multiple outfits. There is no reason she should have looked like that. He never kept her again.

A year later, I was laid off from my job and my daughter and I relocated to back to St. Louis. Work was easier to find there. I still tried to keep the window of communication open with my daughter's father so she could have a relationship with him. He was consistent for a few weeks and then he dropped out of her life. She was devastated. She started acting up in school, her grades fell, and she cried all the time. She was in the third grade. I took her to see a counselor for a year. It broke my heart to know that she was going through this. I wanted her to know she was a blessing and loved from the moment she entered this world. I wanted her to know regardless of how rejected she felt by her father, it was not her fault. I tried to bring as much family around her as I could. My mother was in a different state, but we spoke almost daily, which made a difference in my daughter's life as she got older. Her brother became a staple she is very much attached to today. I wanted to prepare her if not shield her from all the heartbreaks of the world. I wanted to protect her from all the insecure monsters who would try to destroy her. I wanted to give her all the knowledge, power, and strength I could instill in her. I wanted her to know God and to lean on Him early in her little life. I wanted her to know when to pray for all, throw a lifeline to some, and jump in for none fearing her drowning too. Go for all your goals because nothing can hold you back but you. I saw all those things when I looked in her little eyes.

At an early age, both of my children took off in their interests. My son with football and my daughter with dance. They pushed themselves to be the best they could be. They are loving and passionate. I never want them to lose that. I encourage them to set continuous goals for themselves annually, that are obtainable. This will always give them something to strive for as they move up to their ultimate goals. My son continued football from little league through his senior year of high school. He later went to college to be a coach/teacher and is completing barber school. My daughter is a beautiful dancer. She has auditioned for a dance company at the studio she takes classes in, high school dance teams and attended conventions where she has won solo performances, and she placed in many other competitions. Through her love for dance, she has discovered choreography is her first love. Had I continued to be in those unhealthy relationships, I would not have been there to help nurture my children to these goals they have achieved in their lives.

— CHAPTER 14 —

Peaceful Road

Going forward, I focused on myself and my children. I remained single for 9 years. My life was a lot more peaceful without relationship drama. I took the time to build my relationship with God and get to know myself. I learned what my interests were and how I wanted my life to be for me and my family. I also looked at why my life had so many dark times. Somewhere inside it felt like I had to be with someone. It was not a sexual thing. I barely enjoyed sex. I learned in my time alone it was lack of connection. I missed connecting with someone who wanted to get to know me. It was not easy. At times I would date, remembering my Mom saying, "you need a husband." However, their true colors were quickly revealed. All the games, lies, and things I did not want to deal with or have around my daughter were the very things I ran into. It was a good thing that I stepped back from relationships because it allowed me to see what I would not have noticed as quickly. It also made me realize how precious the time to myself was. I enjoyed my peace and quiet. It was the first time in a long time I did not have my joy stolen by someone putting me down, compromising myself to make someone else feel better, or worrying if they are cheating and lying. I will admit sometimes I would watch a movie or see something on social media pertaining to happy, in love couples and I would wonder should I be back out there? Then I remembered how far I had come. How far I had been delivered. I dealt with depression for years. There were several times I was suicidal. In those dark lonely moments in my life I was trying to understand why my life was like it was. For years, I did not believe God loved me and I was angry at him. I did not ask for all the pain and hurt I went through. I only wanted to love someone and to be loved. These guys treated me like I was nothing. I was expendable to them. Easy to be used and tossed away because they did not know what they wanted. There was so much disappointment in them and me. I kept putting myself in those situations. I remembered all I had to deal with any time I opened that door. It made me feel as though everyone is not meant to be in a relationship and I was okay with that. In the years I was alone, I studied God's word, and I learned I was wrong. I always had God's love and I had to learn to love myself.

When I look back on all the years of pain I endured, that time was nothing compared to what I had gained in my singleness. I was free to focus on my children and their needs. I did not feel torn between dating someone and putting in time with my children. For me, there was not a question. My children came first. That was always my mindset. I thought I was doing that over the years but through my bad decisions my children suffered. I grew to appreciate the life God gave me. I learned that I was enough. My children were enough. Most importantly, God was enough. I was there for my daughter and all her activities. I was there to help with homework, movie nights and getting her ready for bed. When my son was younger, we had special outings and movie days. As he got older, I was available for deep talks with my son that helped him and his friends. I was flexible to use my weekends to drive up to his school to hang out for a day. Or for the family to hit the highway for a weekend getaway. I did not have to answer to anyone but God. It was the most peace and freedom I had felt in my life.

Would I ever be in another relationship? Only if it is God's will. I used to joke that, *"Jesus would have to tap me on the shoulder Himself and say, that is the one."* To be honest, that is exactly what He did. I had been reunited with my high school sweetheart. This is something I never thought would happen. I could not imagine being in a relationship with anyone, especially not with the guy from high school. Although we kept in touch here and there over the years, we were always friends no matter what. I knew him to be married for over 20 years. Now I do not know about you, but in my fairytale bubble, that's a couple that stays together forever.

Unfortunately, their marriage was not my fairytale, and our union was not one either.

When he called me to tell me he was getting a divorce, I thought it was a joke. When he explained further, I was angry and hurt. I know it seems weird, but I was rooting for them, like all my married friends who had long term relationships. As the months went on, we kept in touch, having deep conversations. I was careful because I did not want to be a rebound. Also, I enjoyed our connection as friends. We talked about everything. He is the only one who really understood me, and I did not want to ruin that. He had options. Once people he knew found out he was single, he was propositioned often. We joked about it. Over time our bond became stronger and one night over watching Stranger Things, we decided to give it another chance. It was rocky at first. We had to work at this. We had a good foundation, but he was careful since he just came out of a relationship. I was concerned on so many levels as well. My first thought was, "Am I supposed to be in a relationship again? If so, is he the one? What about our children?" My reservations ran deep. I was asking myself could I do this. Was he ready after being in a marriage for so long? Then I stopped spiraling and took all those questions to God. We are both cautious people, so it has been a long journey of getting to know one another again and trusting God to bring us through. We were both defensive. Trigger words were like bombs to us. We took all our past frustrations and fears out on one another. We did not believe we would make it and almost gave up a few times. When we started to communicate better, we dug through the mess of our past and focused on what was the root of our problems. We felt unlovable and we held our baggage tight. We had to let it all go and remember what we meant to one another. We discovered years ago, God brought us together and we were not mature enough to handle that relationship. We have been blessed with a second chance and have been taking our time to do it the right way. I have grown a lot in this relationship, and it has all been worth it. We are not perfect, but we are for one another. He pushes me where I need it, I support him where he needs it, we pray together on all things and as the days go by, we get better.

He does not try to tear me down or belittle me. He encourages and lifts me up. He wants to see me succeed in what I want to do. This is a different kind of relationship because I do not feel I have to worry about all those immature, petty things I used to in the past. Our children have accepted and given their blessing to this union. That meant the most to me. I finally feel like I have achieved a next-level relationship that only God could provide. I was not looking or asking for this. God provided this for me and gave me the family I have always wanted. We know the secret to keeping this union together is staying close to God.

After a couple of years of working on us, he proposed on Christmas morning with all our children involved. They all held up signs saying "Kris, will you marry me?" I turned to find my first love down on one knee. I cried. I was so happy. In that moment I knew I was lovable because the first man who ever loved me still did. And to prove it, 6 months later he made me his Mrs.

CHAPTER 15

Released

My experiences have always kept me from excelling in life. I became a victim of my circumstances. I allowed my past to dictate my future. I believed those scars on the inside were permanent. When I reconnected with God, I connected what I did not understand as a little girl, to what I now understand as an adult. All those things I told myself were lies. Those scars were not permanent. Through His stripes, I am healed. Completely. He forgave me for all my indiscretions. I had not forgiven myself. It healed the 13-year-old girl who was raped. She knows God did not abandon her. She knows God never stopped loving her. One of my favorite songs is by Tasha Combs Leonard 'You Still Love Me.' It helped me to see He was by my side the whole time. Through every abusive situation, through every heartbreak,

I was not alone. When I came to Him instead of running to create another problem, He released me. He released my pain. Most importantly, He taught me how to forgive. It is possible to overcome your obstacles. It is possible to overcome your past. It is possible to obtain peace and happiness while in a healthy relationship. The moment I had my breakthrough, I knew my testimony is one I needed to share to help others. It did not matter if I was a private person. It did not matter how people would view me. What mattered is encouraging other women who have walked a similar path.

I began my own nonprofit to work with domestic violence survivors. I was invited to speak at holiday events hosted in domestic violence centers. I was moved that my story helped others. I had to help them realize that God brought you through your situation for a reason. Many women never make it out. If He brought you through, your work is not done. Seek Him and find your purpose. After talking with these ladies, I knew I had to do something on a larger scale, and I started putting together a podcast for women empowerment. It is for women of all ages. I encouraged my daughter to be involved as well. It is important to train our children at a young age to serve the Lord. All this work is unto God because if I continue to honor Him in all I do, I will continue to have a peaceful road on this journey of continuous release.

Made in the USA
Monee, IL
10 November 2020